NATION FIRST

Shikha Akhilesh Saxena is an IT professional, entrepreneur, educator and a mother of two children. After her husband, Captain Akhilesh Saxena, sustained injuries during the Kargil War, the couple was forced to restart their lives. Sheer dedication and an unwavering spirit explain their success: Akhilesh is now Vice President at Tata Communications, while Shikha is the founder and CEO of Inspiring Mantras, which conducts leadership programmes.

Praise for the book

'What makes this book unique is that it's written from a wife's perspective, so her book cuts through military jargon to describe the battles of Tololing and Three Pimples where her husband, Captain Akhilesh Saxena, fought and was critically wounded. While her husband battled the enemy, she had to fight off her own anxieties...[but] both of them overcame their respective physical and mental challenges and came out as winners. ...A must-read for those who want to know more about the Kargil Conflict...the personal accounts of the battles of Tololing and Three Pimples, and hear the story of people left behind at home when a soldier goes off to fight for his country.'

– B.S. Dhanoa, Air Chief Marshal (Retd.)

'An electrifying and moving account of courage seen not just through the eyes of braveheart Captain Akhilesh Saxena, war-wounded hero of Kargil, but also through the eyes of his wife who was no less than a soldier at the frontline. The book is a must-read and takes you through a gamut of emotions with its extraordinary and intimate portrait of what happens to a family when a soldier comes home from war and when the headlines have faded. I hope everyone reads this book to understand the emotions that maketh a man and his home. Highly recommend this book.'

– Barkha Dutt, Journalist and Author

'The wife of an army officer writes this touching memoir, giving a fresh perspective of the '99 war. The tale of a warrior is incomplete without recognizing the emotional being inside him. *Nation First* brings to life the bloodiest battles without losing sight of the tenderness of humanity. Shikha's story is one of incomparable grit, determination and perseverance, that is sure to inspire!'

– Anupam Kher, Actor, Producer and Director

'One's life unfolds in proportion to one's courage. Shikha's heart-wrenching memoir *Nation First* will inspire a new generation of young men and women to join the forces. It is a first-hand account of the impact on families and partners of war heroes and soldiers who themselves pay a heavy price for this supreme duty. *Nation First* is about putting the soldier first, the family first and the heart first. It is a glimpse of the journey of a woman who truly epitomizes the saying, "when the going gets tough, the tough get going."'

– Dr Annurag Batra, Chairman BW Businessworld and Founder exchange4media

'One can only read this with tears, pride and patriotism. A tribute to valour and courage.'

– Anand Neelakantan, Author of *Asura: Tale of the Vanquished* and Bahubali trilogy

NATION FIRST

SHIKHA AKHILESH SAXENA

hachette
INDIA

First published in India in 2023 by Hachette India
(Registered name: Hachette Book Publishing India Pvt. Ltd)
An Hachette UK company
www.hachetteindia.com

2

Maps on pp. 113–14 illustrated by Neelima P Aryan
Army icon illustrated by Nihar Apte

ISBN 978-93-5731-166-3

Hachette Book Publishing India Pvt. Ltd
4th & 5th Floors, Corporate Centre,
Plot No. 94, Sector 44, Gurugram – 122003, India

Typeset in Sabon LT Std
by Jojy Philip, New Delhi – 15

Printed and bound in India
by Manipal Technologies Limited

MIX
Paper from responsible sources
FSC™ C043100

The glory of the young legends that the Kargil range knows,
Where the wind softly sings and cool breeze blows.
They sing the stories of the brave lads of long ago,
The springs from the great glacier still gently flow.
But they weep sadly for the brave who roar no more,
These high mountains are the witnesses of the Kargil War,
Where our soldiers climbed, in the fire shower, amidst the snow,
With their heads held high, marching forward to face the foe.
No fear, no consternation could stop their determined aim,
They achieved an impossible victory with their incredible game.
There is peace and freedom again, where once there was war,
Quiet and calm surroundings wherever you can see so far.
Celebrate independence but remember, they couldn't be cured,
Sacrificed their lives or body parts, so our
well-being was ensured.
Leaving every Indian with pride, some soldiers
now sleep among the stars,
And some, with their families, still live with
the war wounds and scars.

CONTENTS

Message from Shri Nitin Gadkari xi
Foreword xiii

Introduction 1
1. Beyond My Horizons 4
2. Rush-Hour Wedding 22
3. Blissful Journey 36
4. A Lady in the Army Regiment 49
5. Posting to Kashmir 66
6. Forward March 77
7. Peaks of Fire 90
8. Battle of Tololing 108
9. The Hump 130
10. Three Pimples Area 145
11. The Last Survival 158
12. Scars, Wounds and a Disabled Officer 171
13. Defeating Misfortune 182
14. Goodbye Uniform 194
15. Re-Attired 207

Letters 217
Acknowledgements 223

MESSAGE FROM SHRI NITIN GADKARI

This wonderful book is all about a true story of a military couple who faced a ruthless Kargil War just after their marriage.

I have read many books on war, but the way Shikha has narrated this electrifying story left me spellbound. This story can only be told by a person who has lived this reality and Shikha does it with great heart. The story of the Kargil War showcases not just the fierce battles fought by the soldiers but the quiet courage shown by their families.

This powerful memoir reminds us that courageous men in uniform are supported by the grace and poise shown by their families. *Nation First* is a remarkable book on the human cost of war and the sacrifices it entails.

A must-read!

Nitin Gadkari
Minister of Road Transport and Highways of India

FOREWORD

Note from General Ved Prakash Malik
(Chief of Army Staff during the Kargil War)

Nation First is the story of Shikha and Captain Akhilesh Saxena, from their marriage, military life in a peace station, and intense battle action of the Kargil War in which Akhilesh was badly wounded, to the experiences of a disabled soldier and building a life of solid standing in the corporate world. Shikha is truly an astute author. With help from Akhilesh, she diligently recounts all factual details so very sincerely: their experiences, including their romance, Akhilesh's emotions when he goes on near-suicide missions in war, the trauma and the travails when he is wounded and hospitalized, and the admirable never-give-up attitude of the young couple. A particularly interesting part of the book is how Akhilesh, as Forward Observation Officer (FOO) supporting the 2 Rajputana Rifles, directed artillery firing during the battles of Tololing, Hump and Three Pimples in the Dras sector. Those exciting battle details make your blood rush even today.

This is truly a first-of-its-kind book. Never have I seen such an inspirational military life story covered in such detail. It is not just a narration of first-hand experience but also an interesting insight into military traditions which build camaraderie, family support, an environment of strong patriotism and our military psychology.

Note from Dr Mrs Ranjana Malik (President of the Army Wife Welfare Association [AWWA] during the Kargil War)

Nation First is one of the most compelling narratives I have come across. From Akhilesh and Shikha's marriage and fairytale romance to his being posted to Kargil soon after, it describes in detail the grim battles and gruesome encounters of the war, as well as his success as an FOO in crucial attacks. This is one of the very few first-person accounts from an officer who, having been involved in battle, survived to tell the tale.

Captain Akhilesh sustained serious injuries to his hand: half his left palm was blown off. Shikha has described his injuries, his mental state, the massive loss of blood, the manner in which he trudged down for hours to get to the base, as well as the painful, difficult years of his hospitalization, repeated surgeries, and physiotherapy while she had to live for over a year in a one-room guest house in the hospital.

As the then-President of AWWA, the narration has left me totally surprised and also ashamed that we did not follow up on what was happening to our wounded officers and soldiers. Our team of volunteers was regularly visiting the hospital, providing help to all those we saw in the wards, in terms of all personal requirements, including emotional counselling and reassurance. I, myself, visited the wards every second day, not only in Delhi but all other military hospitals in Leh, Kargil, Srinagar and Bareilly as well. I was there when the famous pianist, Brian Silas, played for the wounded soldiers in the hospital. Patients were brought out on wheelchairs and beds. Captain

Akhilesh visiting the soldiers in other wards to reassure his colleagues tore a hole in my heart.

It was heart-rending to read of his decision to leave the army for a civilian life, and moved me to tears, yet the end was so very heart-warming in every way. A disabled officer, after leaving the army (with a heavy heart) tops his MBA and begins a successful career. Every step of the way, every successful job, he credits his army training, having used the lessons from the Kargil war for corporate management.

A large part of the credit for his success and his achievements, undoubtedly, goes to his wife, Shikha, who stood by him like a rock, encouraging him throughout. She did not let him lose heart, and was by his side through thick and thin.

This narration of their life story has touched me deeply. I wonder how many of us realize the true potential of our officers and men, and how brilliantly they perform when life takes them along a different path. Also, the strength of character of the army wife, who sees her husband go to battle and welcomes him back with open arms. This truly takes a lot of courage, tenacity and mental strength.

INTRODUCTION

A tribute to our Indian soldiers and their families; they are role models for the people of India.

'Bare mountains, no sight of trees or rocks to hide behind. All our movements were under observation by the enemy sitting above us on the mountain peaks. It was the most challenging terrain for a soldier to face when the consequence of death seemed certain.'

Let me take you down memory lane to the year 1999: the year of the Kargil War. I heard all the stories from the most authentic source, my husband, Captain Akhilesh Saxena. I still don't know how he survived that shower of bullets and bombs. The battles were fought on the mountain peaks of Kargil, and the resounding victories rejuvenated nationalism and pride in our countrymen.

Unfortunately, very few officers who led the attack from the front are alive to present the true picture of the assault. Capt. Akhilesh took part in three attacks: the battles of Tololing peak, Hump area and Three Pimples area. He fought alongside an infantry unit as Artillery Forward Observation Officer (FOO), as part of the assault team of 2 Rajputana Rifles. He directed the massive firing of 120 artillery guns on Tololing peak when our soldiers fought like an undefeated army, and India gained its first victory in the Kargil War. Capt. Akhilesh shared war moments with Major P. Acharya, Major Vivek Gupta, Capt. Vijayant

Thapar and Capt. Vikram Batra. By the grace of God, even after being hit by Pakistan's artillery shelling, he survived to tell inspiring tales of the war and draw an accurate picture of what transpired. He laid it all out: the operation planning on the battlefront, as well as the mental status, emotions and interactions within the Indian troops who marched forward on the peaks for the suicide mission.

I spent many months at the hospital in 1999, sitting by the bedside of my wounded husband, who often woke up in agony in the middle of the night. During those sleepless nights, he narrated to me the terrors of the war zone. In addition to his recollections, I collated stories from my meetings with Air Chief Marshal B.S. Dhanoa, Brigadier Amrinder Singh Kasana, Colonel M.B. Ravindranath and many other friends and soldiers of the Indian Army.

I was from a civilian background, with no ties to the armed forces, when I married Capt. Akhilesh two months before the Kargil War broke out. This book traces the emotions of a military couple facing a ruthless war immediately after their wedding. It is a peek into our lives in the armed forces environment, and reflects the values and traditions of the Indian Army. It shows how a civilian girl gathered the courage to face the brutal truth of war and its repercussions in society. It highlights the role and life of a soldier's wife in the Indian Army. It showcases how an officer survived severe war injuries, and it also delves into the dilemmas faced by a disabled soldier. It reveals how a couple battled the situation they were thrown into, and how a severely wounded and disabled officer emerged to take on a new role in the corporate world, proving his ability to work in the professional multinational space. Capt. Akhilesh now has a successful and fulfilling career as Vice President at Tata Communications. And I am a mother of two grown-up kids, driven by my passion for sensitizing civilian society to the values of the armed forces. Our life is just one example of the many lives in the armed forces; fighting against and defeating uncertain situations. We have lived every moment mentioned in the book. However, some names and identifying details have been changed to protect the privacy of the people involved, and the details of some events have been altered/recreated to protect sensitive information.

BEYOND MY HORIZONS

No, I really didn't know what I was getting into.

The sky appeared like a deep navy blue-black silk cloth, and the stars were like scattered diamonds glittering on that cloth. The moon seemed like a shimmering silver orb hanging in the lonely sky. At the height of 16,000 feet, it deceived one into believing they could touch the glowing moon just by standing on their toes. Rays of moonlight, as bright as diamond flare, set the Drass valley aglow like melted platinum. There was a spectacular display of stars. Unlike night skies in other parts of the world, where an electric glow allows only a few constellations to shine through, here, the firmament flickered with millions of lights. At midnight, there was visibility even in the dark cerulean glow. One's sight could travel for miles, as there were no obstacles in the way. The barren, rocky mountains, with no shrubs or trees, resembled an arid desert. The sound of the Sura River flowing at the base of the hills was easily audible.

As one's sight sneaked down, one could see a grey cloud cast over the ground like a big net. Suddenly, hundreds of golden fireballs appeared in the sky, turning everything to ash wherever they dropped. The thunder of heavy artillery gun shelling shook the mountain, and the vibrations of the explosions travelled for miles. The smell of gunpowder filled the air, and the lack of oxygen made it tougher to breathe. Under the shower of fire, the silhouettes of two army men emerged from the shadows, trudging downhill. In the mountains, the trail is never straight. They stumbled a few times because of the irregular surface. Unaware of the correct direction, every step they took towards the medical camp was a gamble. They set out with measured strides, their inner compasses fixed on invisible coordinates that led them towards the nearest medical post. Both looked terribly exhausted with dirty, black faces and chapped lips. Their ragged uniforms looked like they had been dragged in the mud and were torn from cuts on their bodies. The patches of blood stains were fresh. One had his hand tied to his head with a small bandage, while blood trickled down his face, soaking his uniform. He was severely injured, and his hand was bleeding profusely. His eyes were getting heavier with each passing minute. Despite being in a critical condition, he had a smile on his face and the conviction that he could live up to the reputation of his uniform, serve his country and fulfil the assigned task. Even though he was hit by the artillery shelling, he had hid his injury and continued fighting with the enemy.

As he walked with trembling legs, his right foot got stuck in a gap between two rocks. He tried to take another step but lost his balance and fell down hard on the rocky surface, getting another cut on his face. He tried standing with one hand but he couldn't manage on his own. His buddy instantly turned and pulled his leg out, stretched his right hand around his own shoulder and helped him stand up. They resumed their journey. The wounded one murmured to himself, 'I have to live.' The image of his beloved appeared in his thoughts, waiting at the railway platform, where he had seen her last. He was struggling hard to breathe and remain conscious, as the continuous bleeding threatened to draw him closer to death. After they had covered a little more distance, his vision got blurry and his legs lost strength; breathing heavily, he fell to the ground and lost consciousness. His buddy quickly took out a bottle and sprinkled water on his officer's face. Holding both his shoulders, he shook him repeatedly hoping to revive him, but got no response. He screamed for help; his voice travelled far into the night but there was no one to hear him.

One-and-a-half months earlier, 12 May 1999.

At 4 a.m., I was standing at the railway station in Moradabad, a small town in Uttar Pradesh. The shadows of the night were still in the sky. There was hardly anyone on the platform; only a few passengers waiting for their trains, sleeping on the benches and floor. I was in his favourite red silk churidar suit crafted with stone sequins and zari. My head was covered with a golden dupatta embedded with hundreds of tiny mirrors, my wrists were adorned with bangles, and toes with rings. I was dressed with every possible auspicious symbol of a newly-wed Indian woman. The crack of dawn was about to spread hope and brightness for everyone, but for me, it seemed like only darkness was left. With every passing moment, my heartbeat was accelerating, and my instincts kept hinting towards some impending doom. The sudden unpleasant changes indicated the approach of a rough phase in our lives. All our plans for the future seemed irrelevant and lost.

My train of thoughts was interrupted as I saw him walking towards me with the ticket in his hand. For a brief while, we stared at each other. I didn't blink even for a fraction of a second, wanting to freeze time. We didn't know when we would see each other again or if I would ever see him again. His sombre eyes expressed the misery he was trying to hide from me. The moments kept slipping from our hands, just like sand. He held my hands and buried his face in my palms as if to inhale the fragrance of henna on my hands. He looked deep into my eyes and said, 'I will call you soon.' Hugging me tenderly, he kissed my forehead.

I smiled weakly to reassure him that everything would be fine. In the next moment, the blaring whistle of the engine left me feeling wretched. He rushed towards the train and left. Suddenly, everything became a blur or perhaps, it was the tears in my eyes. My heart wanted to stop him, but my mind knew it was impossible. I watched the train leaving the platform until it disappeared. I didn't want to leave the station; I wanted to accompany my husband wherever he was going. It had been only two months since I started a happy married life as a new bride. And at that moment, the train had taken all my dreams, and my future away. To make matters worse, society's conservative beliefs were adding to my edginess, tagging me an unlucky bride. My self-confidence was shaken, my heart was sinking, and I silently prayed for the well-being of my husband. Tears rolled down my cheeks as the gravity of the situation hit me.

Kashmir, one of the most beautiful locations in India, this heaven on earth, was now considered one of the most challenging postings in the defence services. Terrorism in Kashmir had tormented the lives of defence personnel. Militants often launched bloody battles to reinforce their separate identities. The neighbouring countries, determined to see turmoil continuing in the Valley, provided training and weapons to the militants. Some people had also been brainwashed or suppressed to the extent that they were willing to support militancy. In such a scenario, our Indian soldiers in Kashmir were like warriors without weapons. They were expected to maintain discipline and peace in the Valley with restricted authority. A portion of civilian society treated defence officers and their families like enemies. They ignored the fact that these army men were willing to go to any extent for the safety of citizens and the honour of the country. Our soldiers were the direct target of stone-pelting incidents, and as a result, security forces and their families felt highly insecure in the Valley.

Capt. Akhilesh received a posting order and was asked to report to duty with just four days' notice. This urgency made me apprehensive about the conditions in Kashmir. It was an unusual call. I shivered, thinking about the discussions I had with a few senior officers' wives of the regiment. 'Nobody gets a posting like this. It indicates an emergency. An officer of the 1889 Light Regiment got injured, and your husband is being called to replace him.' 'This rarely happens. Generally, they wait for a posted officer to recover.' 'What is the urgency? Why is the army deploying more officers in that area? The situation there must be getting worse.'

The information about suspicious militancy movement near the northern Line of Control seemed solid. Some terrorists had even occupied the Indian army bunkers. The ridges of Kargil, Mushko Valley, Drass, Batalik and other sectors were under red alert. The Indian Army could possibly pass orders to all the regiments of Kashmir to move towards that area. In the initial weeks leading up to May 1999, some local shepherds reported seeing some tall, well-built men near the forward military post at Kargil. They were not wearing army uniforms, but dressed in long kurtas and pyjamas. They were most likely militants, as local people noticed guns slung on their shoulders. These suspicious men were living inside the bunkers vacated by Indian soldiers the previous winter, as had been the usual practice followed by the Indian Army as well as Pakistani Army every year since 1971. With temperatures dropping to –50 degrees centigrade during winter, human survival is extremely arduous and expensive on these peaks. So, on both sides of the LOC, Indian and Pakistani soldiers would come down from their forward-observation posts. These were known as the winter-vacated posts. But that year, locals observed movement at the posts much before the Indian regiments could reoccupy their bunkers. It was like somebody from outside had seized the opportunity and established their authority in an unoccupied house.

I stood on the platform like a statue, staring at the long gone train. I could not move until my brother-in-law said, '*Bhabhi... ghar chalo...*' (Sister-in-law, let's go home). I looked at him, wanting to convey my pain, but felt too overwhelmed to speak. With a heavy heart, I quietly sat behind him on the scooter and returned home. At home, my mother-in-law and father-in-law tried to keep themselves busy with their work. I could sense the silence and emptiness everywhere. The place that used to be filled with laughter had become deserted. That afternoon, although everyone was present at the lunch table, nobody ate anything. Their minds were somewhere else. It seemed as if the smiles of my family members had faded with Akhilesh's departure.

It was a sad night. I couldn't sleep. Memories kept me awake. I remembered the day my father came from Meerut to meet me in Dehradun for an unusual conversation. Unusual because I had never had a personal discussion with him earlier, he had always been devoted to his official duties. I was close to Ma and shared all my secrets with her. She was my best friend and adviser. My father, Dr Rajendra Prasad, and my mother, Dr Vedwati Prasad, were posted as the Chief Medical Officer (CMO) and Chief Medical Superintendent (CMS) respectively, at the government hospital in Meerut. My entire life, I had seen them prioritize the well-being of their patients. Being government employees, they never set up private practices as it went against their principles. I used to live in Dehradun with my elder brother Vishal, who had been my partner-in-crime since birth. We made the best team and always won any game in the neighbourhood. As soon as I completed my management in information technology, I skipped the campus interviews to join him in establishing our own business and took charge as the director and centre head of the Arena Multimedia education franchise centre in Dehradun. We worked hard together to make our institute one of the best in the north zone. I was an ambitious girl, but deeply attached to my family. As I admired my mother a lot, I always wanted to be an earning member like her and be available to my family, balancing life perfectly. By this time, I had started earning well, was independent and happy, yet not satisfied. Impressed by my parents, I wanted to serve the people of my country, so I started offering free computer classes for underprivileged kids. Things were moving at their pace, when one day, Papa came from Meerut and took me out for a drive. It was the first time he spoke to me like a friend and shared his worries.

'I will retire next year, and it's my wish to get you married while I am still in service. Right now, I have friends and resources to organize it well. If you decide early, it would be of great help. But if you want to decide after a year, then too I will do my best, but it would be an arduous task for me to arrange everything.' I realized he was right. My parents wanted me to get married, and I didn't want to leave them feeling stressed.

In the third week of December 1998, my parents took us for a tour of south India. We visited several coastal towns and well-known temples: Suryanar Kovil temple, Rameshwaram and Kanyakumari. My heart sought blessings from the Goddess for my unknown future husband. When we returned to Meerut, my father's secretary handed him a box filled with letters. It contained replies to the matrimonial advertisement he had placed in the newspaper before embarking on the trip. Papa promptly handed the box over to my mother, and Ma asked me to stay with her in Meerut while she responded to the letters.

On a chilly January night, Ma and I were sitting under the quilt with the heater on in the room. Located in a corner of the Meerut Cantonment, this bungalow was of the pre-

Independence era. The British had built houses for their executives in or near the cantonment as it was considered the most posh area of any town. The house contained many enormous rooms with high ceilings, surrounded by a garden and a lush green field that ran into acres, and had a half-kilometre pathway from the gate to the porch. I was going through the proposals when I found one from Moradabad. Their son was in the Indian Army. He was expected to come home for a two-week vacation, and they wanted to meet us during that time. I tried to get Ma's attention, but she was busy reading other letters. I tried again, but her reaction was the same. Instead, she showed me a picture of a software engineer working for Infosys, who was on his way to the United States.

'He is the right match for you as you are in IT, and he is also in the software industry. Both of you will grow well together.' She smiled affectionately and continued, 'There are other excellent options too. One is an IAS officer, and the other is working for Star Plus. I think Delhi would be the perfect location for you, as you will have ample opportunities to grow professionally.'

I spent the whole night thinking. It was time for me to understand my priorities and figure out what I wanted in my life partner. Life was offering me the choice of a settled married life, assured career growth and the opportunity to settle abroad. But still, these were not enough for me to decide, as I was looking for something else.

In the morning, I drew Ma's attention to the Moradabad proposal. 'I want to marry an army officer,' I blurted out.

Mother asked me with concern, 'Do you know anything about the army?'

'No.'

She said, 'I have a basic impression of their lives. One of my friends married an army officer, but he barely lived with her. He was always on duty, and my friend handled everything herself. The situations army wives have to deal with are not normal. They lead a nomadic life, moving from station to station, or are separated from their husbands for long periods and live in constant fear when their husbands are posted to volatile areas. Will you be able to live like this, away from your husband most of the time?'

The question was practical. I remained quiet as I had no answer. It's true that civilians are apprehensive about choosing the armed forces as a career option or getting their daughters married to defence personnel. We look forward to marriage as a settlement, where the couple is dedicated to each other and supports each other even in the small moments of life. *How is all that possible while living apart? I don't want to wait for my husband most of the time and live alone. Then, what would be the point of marrying someone?* My thoughts continued to ramble.

After a couple of days of thinking, I still found myself drawn towards having an army man as my life partner. The man in the olive green uniform, dedicated to the service of the nation was above any other profession for me. I wanted an honest, wise, brave and kind-hearted person, and I somehow believed I could find this rare combination in an army officer. I firmly presumed that soldiers are the most sincere people, because of my close friend, Neetu. She was the daughter of an army officer and had married one as well. Her father wasn't around most of the time when we were growing up. *If that organization is so uncertain and miserable, why do they make new relationships and bonds within the same fraternity? What is so satisfying that they keep serving the nation from generation to generation?'* I was an outsider to the army and caught a glimpse of their lives only when I visited Neetu at her home. They were not rich but were content and happy people, and were greatly respected in society. No one can deny that theirs is the most sincere workforce in the nation. Though life in the defence services is challenging, the pride in serving the nation cannot be rivalled. This feeling is not just among officers, but extends to family members too. Marrying an army person was the opportunity for me to enter the armed forces world. Maybe this was the satisfaction I was looking for.

I had another conversation with Ma. This time, I was clear and well-prepared. 'Ma, when a soldier leaves his family and goes on field postings, he is alone there, away from the comfort of home and affection of family. He does this as his duty and for the security of our country. If he can prioritize service to the nation, why can't I sacrifice his presence around me for the same reason? It will be an opportunity to serve my country with my life partner. Your friend was brave to marry a soldier. I want to be a woman who stands strongly behind my soldier, supports him and loves him with all my heart. I respect army officers the most and want to share my life and heart with one. Like any armed forces personnel, I will also place my nation first, above me and my comfort.' I took a pause just to see Ma's reaction and continued, 'A soldier is also a citizen. In fact, the highest obligation and privilege of citizenship is bearing arms for one's country. It will be a proud privilege to be the wife of an army officer who leads a life of discipline and self-respect.' I quickly added, 'Please, Ma, I promise, I will not complain or regret the life I am choosing.' At that moment, I had no clue that time would test me soon enough. And it would not be easy to perform the role of an army wife.

I could see that Ma was still not entirely convinced, yet she agreed to consider officers from the armed forces, for my sake.

On the morning of 16 January 1999, the three of us got ready to visit Moradabad. My parents had agreed to meet Capt. Akhilesh Saxena and his family. His father, Chandra Prakash Saxena, was a retired labour officer and his mother, Chandra Kanta Saxena, was a school teacher in Moradabad. Soon, our car was zooming on the highway. Despite all the confidence and sane thoughts in my mind, deep within, I was an insecure girl who feared marriage. I never understood the concept of arranged marriage. *How could one decide if someone was their soulmate in just one or two meetings? But then, even after many interactions, one could still misjudge a person.* So I decided that the choice would be mine, but the decision would be my parents'. I could make a mistake, but my parents would not; after all, they were more mature and experienced. I wanted some measure to judge the right person, so I decided to tell them that I didn't know cooking, as I didn't want someone to marry me just to carry out household chores. My unsettled thoughts were reflected in the nervousness on my face, which Ma observed easily. Holding my hand, she smiled and said, 'Don't worry, everything will be okay.'

After the four-hour journey, we reached Hotel Mansarover Paradise, in the heart of Moradabad. Papa had booked a room there so we could speak comfortably. It was a small room with a sofa on one side and a double bed on the other. He arranged for two more chairs. Meanwhile,

I quickly checked my makeup in the washroom mirror. I tried to smile a few times, but the stress was clearly evident on my face. I got time to settle down as they arrived 20 minutes later.

Capt. Akhilesh was of average height, dark complexioned and with impressive looks. There was a spark in his eyes and he sported a permanent gentle smile that was contagious. He was wearing a light turquoise coat. As he entered the room with his parents, he greeted my parents and smiled at me. We received them warmly and exchanged namastes. His father sat next to mine. He was a friendly and down-to-earth person who immediately started talking to Papa. Ma offered his mother a seat beside us. She was a sober lady and quite disciplined in her gestures. She was extremely measured in how she spoke and barely smiled. I was quiet, and Akhilesh appeared to be cheerful and talkative. He told us he was an artillery officer and explained a little about the army. His engaging conversation brought a smile to everyone's face.

After a while, he came by my side and said, 'Do you want to ask something?'

'I know nothing about army life,' I responded.

'That's okay. I will tell you everything. Anything else?'

'I don't know how to cook.'

He burst into laughter and said, 'That's not a problem. We have an officers' mess in the army. We can both eat there.' That answer brought a smile to my face.

While returning, it was dark and foggy outside, and there was poor visibility on the road. The driver had a tough time driving us home safely. The situation inside me was no different. I could not comprehend my feelings or assess Akhilesh's views about our meeting.

Two days later, Papa told us that his family wanted to meet us again. We invited them for lunch. It was 22 January 1999. Although we had two cooks to prepare the meal, I cooked fish at Ma's behest. This time, I chose to wear a royal-blue velvet suit with an embroidered, white net dupatta. Ma hugged me and said, 'You are looking magnificent, my adorable doll. Nobody can remain unimpressed by your graceful smile and attractive eyes. He will surely like you,' she added, 'Just leave your hair open.' She removed the black clip from my hair and gently smoothened it. Slowly, she parted my hair and placed one side in the front, on my shoulder, while leaving the rest behind. I smiled and felt confident.

Around noon, my parents received our guests in the drawing room. Behind the curtains of the next room, the dining hall, I tried hard to hear the conversation, but because of the vast space they were not clearly audible. After a while, Ma called me into the drawing hall. This time, his younger brother, Neeraj, was also with them. Akhilesh's eyes were continuously staring at me. Every time our eyes met, I blushed a deep shade of red. I sensed a warm sensation on my cheeks and soon disappeared back into the dining hall.

Ma came to me and asked, 'Do you like him? They want to do the engagement right now. They have come prepared with a beautiful ring for you.'

I got butterflies in my stomach and blurted, 'But, Ma, it is too early.'

She explained, 'He has to go back to his regiment and cannot return soon. So, they want to decide right now. Your father and I find him to be the perfect army officer for you, just as you desired.'

I was confused and thought it was too early to make a decision. With an indecisive mind, I headed to the market with Ma to buy a ring for Akhilesh. Before I could get to know the man, I was engaged to him. The only solace was that he was an army officer. Even before I knew it, we were entering into a life-long commitment. And the name *Captain Akhilesh Saxena* had become an indispensable part of my life.

At lunch, I discovered he doesn't eat fish, which was the first dish I prepared for him. I hardly knew anything about him. I wanted more time to understand him better. But destiny had other plans. Papa asked me to take him for a walk. After taking him around the house, we sat down in my room. We had about five minutes together as personal moments. He asked for a photograph of mine that he could carry with him. I took out my album, handed it over to him, and said, 'Take whichever one you like.'

'You can keep one or two if you like, I am taking the rest with me,' he replied.

I looked at him and saw that he was smiling, which made me blush. I was amazed to see him display a loving sense of ownership over me within a few moments of our togetherness.

Two days later, he called to inform me that he was returning to his artillery regiment.

I asked, 'What is an artillery regiment?'

'So, the Indian Army is divided into different arms and services. Infantry regiments are soldiers with small arms, the artillery regiment has massive guns, and the armoured regiment has big tanks. These are the fighting arms,' he replied.

I was trying to comprehend what he explained, but it bounced over my head.

'I work with the massive guns. You really know nothing about the army?'

'No, I don't have any relatives in the army. You are the first one.'

'Impressed by the army uniform?' he asked mischievously.

'Yes, and I know that these men are good at taking orders,' I replied, adding my own twist.

He burst into laughter. Noticing he was in a lighter mood, I eagerly asked him, 'How did you make this decision about us? As I don't know anything about the army. It is an altogether different world for me.'

He paused and then replied, 'I liked you at first sight as it felt as though you were the one I was looking for. I admire your beauty and honesty, which is reflected in your every word. Your beautiful, innocent eyes captured my mind. Now, whenever I close my eyes, I see you.' I blushed as if some bright, beautiful glow had lit my face. I could perceive his love and commitment. That five-minute meeting in my room and a single phone call got fixed in my memory. I understood that the secret of having a beautiful relationship doesn't depend on a love marriage or an arranged one. It is based on the firm commitment and care two people give each other.

The very next day, his National Defence Academy (NDA) course-mate Captain Raghvinder Budhwar came to meet me as he was posted in the Meerut Cantonment. Ma offered him tea with hot pakoras and a plate full of laddoos. I got my first lessons from him; even before knowing about Akhilesh's family, the army or married life, I understood the bond of course-mates.

'Nobody knows your fiancé better than us. We have survived the toughest days of our life together. In the NDA, course-mates explore all the possible options to survive punishment and have fun. We are from Echo-Squadron, also known as Eagles, destined to run. The Cross(X)-Country was a significant event, it was a matter of prestige for Eagles to win the trophy, Glider. Every Sunday, we would practice with sincerity and dedication, taking the full route. Based on the performance of the run itself, we were allowed 'liberty'. Liberty means on Sunday you can leave the campus and go to Pune, spend the entire day as you like and indulge in masti (fun) with friends. It was like a dream to first- and second-term cadets, because even if you have done exceptionally well, the privilege is not guaranteed. But when we were in the second term, Akhilesh was understudy to the squadron cadet captain, and somehow managed to get the liberty slip for us every Sunday. We were famously known as *Chandal Chaukari* (name given to these four mischievous cadets by their course mates). Akhilesh, Deven, Bala and I would slip out of the academy after the run, and much before breakfast, to watch movies and eat a lot of parathas at my parent's place in Pune. One Sunday, the squadron performance was bad and liberty was cancelled for everyone. It was announced at breakfast, but by then we were in Pune, unaware of the orders. When we returned at night, everyone was waiting for us. The seniors scolded Akhilesh and like a true friend, he took all the responsibility. But we all fell in and were punished for the entire week. We had a good time though, so no regrets. Akhilesh is a dare devil, and a true friend.'

By the time he finished the story, he had eaten all the laddoos on the plate. While leaving he said, 'It was important for me to see whether or not my brother is at the right place.'

'So, is your brother at the right place?' I asked.

'He is Chatak (clever) Saxena, and has always made the right decisions,' Capt. Budhwar said with a smile. 'Shikha, you have a house in every corner of the country, any course-mate will always welcome you with warmth. We are bonded for life.' It was like a blessing and an assurance from a friend on behalf of all the other friends who had not even met me. I was thrilled and felt lucky.

'Some roads are meant to be walked upon only with a companion!' These words were the opening line of the card I received from Akhilesh within a week, accompanied by a teddy bear and flowers. I also got a photograph of him wearing the Indian Army uniform, from his parents. The threads of love were slowly being woven together with this stranger. I began to smile all the time, for no particular reason. I had never felt so content and at peace before. I just wanted these moments to continue for a long time. I wanted a long courtship to prepare myself better for the new relationship with him and the army. After all, that was the place I would have to fit into. I travelled back to Dehradun and got involved in my daily routine at the institute, but now, I would wait for his call at the end of the day. In those days, only a few of us had mobile phones, and the landline phone was only at my institute. I started staying late at the institute, as Akhilesh would call me at night. Engrossed in our talks, we lost all sense of time. And slowly, I got introduced to the whole new world of army vocabulary.

RUSH-HOUR WEDDING

The moments of happiness we enjoy take us by surprise. It is not that we seize them, but that they seize us.

It was a beautiful Sunday morning in Dehradun. I was in the small garden outside our home. The fragrance of flowers permeated the cool air, there was a carpet of natural grass below my feet, and the warmth of the sun revived me with energy for the entire week. On weekdays, I only got to see the lush forest as a wallpaper on my computer screen while sitting in an air-conditioned room at my institute.

I saw my landlord's daughter coming towards me. 'There is a call for you.' She raised her voice from a distance. 'From a Capt. Akhilesh?' she added quizzically.

'He is my fiancé, serving in the Indian Army,' I said, smiling softly. I had not told anyone about the engagement, but people around gradually noticed the gold ring that covered almost half of my ring finger.

'You didn't tell me you are engaged. Oh! Now, I notice your ring. Congratulations,' she said, gazing at it.

I lived with my brother in a small, rented house. The landlord lived next door and we shared the same garden. Though I had a mobile phone, a massive black Nokia from those days, the network connection was not very good. When the institute was closed on Sundays, my parents connected with me on the landlord's landline. I assumed he had taken the number from them.

It was 7 February, just two weeks after my engagement. He informed me, 'I will not be calling you for a few weeks as I am going for training with my regiment, and there is no network connectivity there.'

'During peacetime, which means no war, we practice with our weapons. That is very important. It is just like preparing for an exam. If we are not prepared, how will we execute at the time of action? We don't know the day of our exam, so we prepare as though *aaj mukabala hoga* (today is the day),' he explained to me.

It was interesting, as I always wondered, *What do army people do when there is no war?*

'Where are you going?' I asked.

'In artillery, we have heavy guns. Their shooting range is about 30 to 40 km, so for practice, we go deep into the deserts of Pokhran or Mahajan in Rajasthan, where there is no civilian population.'

'What! How will you live there? Do you have a setup in the desert?'

He laughed. 'No, we will carry everything from kitchen equipment to guns. We start from scratch and set up all the tents.' Then he asked me softly, 'Is it okay if I do not call you?'

An effortless smile appeared on my lips. I whispered, 'I like when you call, but if it's not possible, then I will wait till you call, no problem.'

I could perceive he was smiling too. 'You sound like an army officer's wife. Welcome to the army.'

The next day was a usual weekday. I knew he would not call. Yet, I waited for his call till late in the evening. Ten p.m. is late for Dehradun, especially during winter. I asked my peon to lock the doors as I packed my bag to go home. Just when I headed outside, the telephone rang. My peon smiled and ran in excitement to open the door. '*Didi, aap ka call aa gaya,* (Didi, that's the call you've been waiting for).'

I picked up the receiver. 'You told me you would not call; it's not possible from the location of your training.'

'Yet you were waiting.' He responded.

I was touched and thought, '*But how did he know I was waiting?*'

'Sweetheart, I am trained to kill I and M from the word IMPOSSIBLE. Everything is possible for me. I just wanted to hear your voice,' he said.

I was surprised. 'But how did you get connectivity?'

'I travelled around 150 km from the desert to the city to find an STD booth to talk to you, and have to travel back 150 km to reach my training area.'

I sensed the depths to which we were connecting, and it felt heavenly. Every moment, I was falling in love with this soldier. Again, we lost all sense of time while talking. At midnight, he reminded me, 'Now, you go home. It is very late and not safe for you.'

'No worries. I will drive down. My house is not far, it will take just 15 minutes by car. But you have to go back to the camp. You will reach around 2 a.m., and you have to be ready for drill at 5 a.m. You will barely get any sleep, so we should end the call.' We softly exchanged good nights and love expressions.

On 10 February, Ma called me, saying, 'We have fixed your wedding for 22 February 1999. Inform Akhilesh as nobody else is in touch with him. He will definitely call you on Valentine's Day.' It sounded like an order. She added, 'You come to Meerut as soon as possible, there is so much to be done.'

I was shocked. 'Ma, it's too early. Please, I wanted a long courtship, which is required to understand each other.' I almost begged.

'Shikha, it is all fixed now since your Papa believes in horoscopes. Panditji said this is the only auspicious date for you to marry Akhilesh this year. And your father doesn't want to wait until next year.'

An Indian wedding requires a lot of planning, and takes weeks and months of preparation. It was hard for me to accept that I would be married in just 12 days. Not even 12 days, as the pre-wedding ceremonies would begin on 18 February, so there was actually only one week to go. *Oh my God, how is it possible? Why such a hurry?* There were so many questions on my mind, but there were no answers. I had to act as instructed by my parents. Their sudden decisions were beyond my understanding. I felt as though we couldn't decide anything; God would take care of everything.

I waited for his call for the next three days, but he did not call. There was too much work to complete before I resigned from my job. I was the only faculty member for 3D applications, and it was my responsibility to finish the course of senior classes, primarily for professionals. So, I started taking back-to-back sessions. Now, most people – family, friends, neighbours, faculty, students, counsellors and peons – were aware of our wedding date, except the groom.

I was sure he would call me on Valentine's Day. Everyone was on alert since the morning. Not only was I waiting for his call, everyone else in the institute was too!

Around 10 a.m., I was surrounded by all the students in the reception sitting area. They wanted a Valentine's Day party. But it was an enormous responsibility, so I was ignoring them. Suddenly, a soldier in uniform appeared at the front door of the institute. He reached the reception desk and inquired about me. The receptionist smiled and pointed me out among the bunch of students. 'There she is, in the pink sari.'

'*Sahab ne yeh aapke liye bheja hai* (My officer has sent this for you).' He handed me a bouquet of lovely red roses. The entire reception area was filled with a pleasant fragrance. All the students stood up and together said, 'We were waiting for you, bhaiyya (brother). Thank you so much.' He left immediately. Now, there was a slight blush and a smile on my face. The students took advantage of the change in my mood.

'Ma'am, please, we want a party in the evening, just for two hours. We will organize everything. You just say yes.' They requested again. This time I could not say no. They all screamed with joy.

They organized a party in the central common area. Everyone was so excited and happy, but my wait was not over yet. I was worried and nervous too. *What if he wouldn't call me today?* It was 8 p.m. and I was sitting next to the phone when it rang.

'I have been hanging around the phone since morning,' I responded with disappointment.

'*Jaaneman, yeh fauj hai, mauj nahin hai* (this is the army, not fun). There is no Sunday or Valentine's Day during army training. Sorry to keep you waiting. I hope you liked the flowers,' he replied cheerfully to make me smile.

'They are beautiful,' I replied. 'Have you received my gifts? I sent them to the address you'd given me. Is this the complete address, or did I miss something? I wrote Captain Akhilesh Saxena, 223 Medium Regiment, C/O 56 APO.'

'Yes, it is complete, don't worry, I will get it when I reach the original regiment location.'

'I have important news...' I was nervous to tell him.

He sensed my nervousness, and said, 'Yes, tell me.'

'Your wedding is on 22 February 1999. Our parents have already dispatched invitation cards to friends and relatives,' I blurted out.

'What! Which date? Are you kidding? My wedding? Our wedding, mine and yours? Please don't crack jokes; it is a shock for me. It's too early.' He was also shocked to hear the date. 'I will not even get leave as they don't let anyone miss training. I doubt I can attend my own wedding.' He was worried, and it reflected in his voice.

'Why don't you call your parents? They wanted to speak to you,' I suggested, hopefully.

'I will,' he said to me and disconnected the call.

I could understand his concerns. He was upset, not with me, but with the situation. Our first Valentine's Day was fraught with uncertainties and unexpected situations. When God plans, you have to surrender. In our lives, the gods were our parents.

I was leaving my job without serving a notice period. There was no time for a farewell party either. The common room was packed with students and employees. It was my last 'lecture'. I addressed everyone, 'When I joined this institute as the centre head, I was much younger than many of my employees and students. I could live up to my designation because I was sincere and hardworking enough to learn whatever was required to carry out my duties. Your actions reflect your image and personality. What you say will be ignored, and what you do will be judged. Do your best, good luck.' They clapped for me for a few minutes; I was aware it was not because of the speech but their association with me.

~

In the deep desert, after the morning drill, Capt. Akhilesh approached his Commanding Officer (CO) of unit 223 Medium Regiment, Colonel V.K. Singh, in his tent.

'Sir, my parents have fixed my wedding for next week, on 22 February. I require leave for my wedding.'

'Oh my God! I thought you were fast, but dammit, you are too fast. How did you manage it sitting in this desert? When do you want to leave?' asked the surprised colonel.

'Tomorrow,' replied the young captain.

'Where is the wedding card?'

'As I haven't seen it yet, I extend my verbal invitation to everyone. I will dispatch the cards for the entire unit as soon as I reach home,' said Akhilesh.

The officers' laughter filled the tent, and everyone congratulated Akhilesh.

~

I reached my parents' home in Meerut on the night of 18 February. The house was beautifully decorated with lights and flowers. It resembled a palace. A few of my relatives had reached before me. It was the first wedding in the family of someone from my generation. Everyone was so excited about the wedding, except for me – I was nervous.

But as I looked at Ma's face, it was radiating happiness. She was busy but looked thrilled. She hugged me and said, 'See how I have managed; I have been collecting things for your wedding over the years. I bought pure silk saris from south India to gift to your in-laws. The only things you have to purchase are the bridal outfits. Tomorrow we will go shopping; there are three ceremonies lined up.'

'Okay Ma, relax now. I am here with you,' I calmed her down.

She smiled and kissed my forehead. 'You just take care of yourself and do a lot of shopping. Your sisters will help you out.' I have two sisters: a sibling, Rachi, and my cousin, Aradhana. The three of us had grown up together, played games, watched movies, sung songs and shared dreams. I don't remember any moments of my childhood without them. That night, we sat together to list all the essential things a bride needs.

In the evening, I received a call from Akhilesh. 'I just reached home. What should I do now? I have nothing to wear on my wedding day. I just have jeans, so I will wear them.'

'Not a problem at all,' I replied immediately, 'I am marrying you, your clothes don't matter to me. But you've reminded me that I too don't have a bridal lehenga to wear on our wedding day, and I still have to purchase one. Without it, I will not be coming for the jaimala (Hindu wedding ritual).' We both laughed.

Hindu weddings are quite elaborate, with several rituals spread out over a few days. On the morning of 20 February, a bus full of relatives and friends of Akhilesh travelled from

Moradabad to Meerut for a ceremony. All my relatives received them, except me, as I was told not to come out until all the guests had settled down in the drawing room after lunch, which was laid out in the garden. I chose to wear Ma's old sari to start my wedding ceremonies. Since childhood, I always wanted Ma for the important events in my life. The fragrance of her being lingered in her clothes and made me feel secure.

I entered the drawing room packed with guests. My tense face relaxed on seeing so many younger siblings and cousins. *These strangers will soon become my family.* The affection in their eyes and smiles on their faces reflected the signs of welcome. We repeated the ring ceremony as no one else besides our parents had been present for the actual one. That day, I had to eat 30 laddoos. Sweets were my least preferred delicacy, but it was tough to say no to the relatives who fed me with a smile.

All the guests left around 6.30 p.m., and my sisters and I ran from the drawing room to swap our saris for jeans. And with our clothes, our attitudes changed as well – from submissive, homely daughters to confident, outgoing girls. We were running late to buy a bridal lehenga. The shopkeeper had already told us he would require one day for the fitting. Papa was waiting in the car, and we rushed towards Abu Lane. In the market, we saw Akhilesh with his brother and father. He too was shopping for the big day. We were too busy to say hello to them, and we all were in jeans, so we just hid and made our way to the shop. Those were the days when girls were supposed to wear only suits or saris in front of their in-laws. They had to leave their parents' homes and adopt all the customs and traditions of their in-laws. Not just this, they had to forfeit their own tastes when it came to dressing. Drastic changes were about to take place, and I realized it the very moment I was hiding from them. A shiver passed through my body with those thoughts, but I ignored it.

Akhilesh called me at night to say, 'We saw you today. It's the first time I've seen you in jeans.' He added, 'You were looking good. Thank God you wear jeans.'

'So, am I allowed to wear jeans when we're married too?' I asked.

'Moradabad is a conservative society and my mother strictly follows the social norms here. I believe you will have to dress only in suits or saris,' he replied, quickly adding, 'But you can wear whatever you like at my regiment. They already know that you were the head of an institute and an IT professional. They are looking forward to welcoming you.' I let out a little sigh of relief.

I understood that I had to play two roles. The family expected a submissive daughter-in-law and Akhilesh wanted a modern, well-educated wife. It was a generation gap; a gap between idealism and practicality. It appears in every generation, sometimes deep, sometimes shallow. Every generation has their own value systems: some they inherit, some they create on their own, and some are altered to suit their requirements. A bride has to maintain a bridge and balance between both generations. The same applies to the groom. The only advantage is that he doesn't have to leave his home and live with his in-laws for the rest of his life. If they support and respect each other, it can be a gradual change; or else it can be hazardous for their relationship. This was the road on which most love stories seemed to lose oxygen.

The next morning, everyone enjoyed applying haldi (a paste of gram flour, turmeric and milk to rejuvenate the bride's skin) on my face. The mehendi (henna) ceremony was planned for the same evening. Some ladies sang and danced to *banni* (bridal folk songs). These songs carry the blessings of elders for the couple to be wed. Suddenly, at 9 p.m., around 20 bikes came to the gate of our residence. The guard sent a message about the bikers. The ladies stopped singing, and everyone was worried. *Who are these bikers, and why had they come?* First, Papa and Vishal went outside. When we heard my father's high-pitched voice, we peeked outside. Oh! The bikers were my students. They all were standing quietly and Papa was scolding them for riding their bikes all the way from Dehradun to Meerut. Finally, he ordered all of them to have dinner after freshening up. After dinner, everyone joined in the singing and dancing. The excitement was multiplied, so much so that no one slept the entire night.

Finally, it was the big day – 22 February 1999 – the wedding day.

The mandap was filled with guests. All the top government authorities of the city, like the district magistrate, commissioner and others, were present in the wedding hall. I was sitting in a room wearing a maroon lehenga-choli with heavy jewellery, poised like a royal Indian diva on the outside but struggling with a turmoil inside. There was a feeling of joy, butterflies in the stomach, a fair share of nervousness, anxiety and fear. So many feelings come together to make you feel like a bag full of diverse emotions. And rightly so, it was a life-changing event. I was instructed not to come out until the baraat (groom's party) arrived. Guests kept coming and going, but there was no trace of the baraat. Most of them went home without meeting the bride and the groom. Around 11.30 p.m., the dhol started, followed by the shehnai. This was the sign that the wait was over, and the baraat was at the doorstep.

'Didi, Jijaji is dancing. The groom is dancing.' One of my little cousins came running to inform me.

Everyone left me inside and ran out to see the groom dancing. In those days, it was a break from tradition to see the groom dance at his wedding. He was expected to keep sitting soberly. Soon, both the groom's side and the bride's side were dancing. Sometimes, it is good to break some rules to spread happiness and liven up the environment. I too wanted to watch him dance, but was helpless as the bride had to maintain a certain decorum.

I appeared like a queen, walking to the stage holding a big garland of roses in my hands, surrounded by my sisters and friends. Akhilesh stretched out his hand to me as I climbed onto the stage. And then the most-awaited moment brought all the relatives closer on the stage, their palms filled with rose petals – the jaimala. Everyone showered petals on both of us. A swing, beautifully decorated with flowers, was arranged on the stage and Akhilesh occasionally swung while we sat on it, as relatives came to greet us.

Slowly, as the ceremonies progressed closer to the time of the kanyadaan (Hindu wedding ritual), I could see sadness and fear settling on Ma's face. This sadness was slowly breaking me as well. She brought me inside the room to change into a yellow sari gifted to me by my mamaji (mother's brother), as per the tradition of the ceremony. Ma started crying, and it impacted me deeply. I felt like a baby who didn't want to leave her parents. Within no time, people around us were crying too. In this scenario, I refused to change my clothes so my mamiji (mama's wife) took out a beautiful yellow dupatta and draped it around me. At that time, I didn't even imagine I was committing a big mistake by not wearing a yellow sari for the kanyadaan.

Kanyadaan is a ceremony in which the bride's parents give her away to the groom. The echo of shlokas (Sanskrit verses) and burning fire in the centre of the mandap created an ultimate sacred environment that tied both of us in a divine bond. We made seven lifetime promises to each other while taking rounds of the havan. Now, the person sitting next to me was no longer a stranger. We both were considered responsible for the happiness and welfare of each other. The presence of elders made this moment gracious.

The night seemed to be just a few moments longer and soon, the rising sun spread brightness all over. But I was nervous; the uncertainty of being in a new house with unknown people was terrifying. Girls are brave, for they face this social ritual gracefully.

I can never forget the words of my father that morning.

He said, 'Beti, now you are married, but that doesn't mean you are no longer part of our family. Instead, we have added Akhilesh to our family. Never think twice about coming home. Your room will always be here in our house. Now you have two houses and many family members, just take care of everyone. I know they are good people, and you will be happy. Still, never hesitate to tell us if you find any threat to you. In no time, I will bring you back. For me, you are so much more important than any social ideology. You go with positivity and confidence. I am sure my daughter will fulfil this new role in her life.'

These words from a father can bring a smile to any daughter's face. The magic of my Papa's words made me walk out with confidence. I wished to create happiness in the lives of my new family members. I took a lot of chocolates for my new brothers and sisters, and gifts for the elders.

BLISSFUL JOURNEY

Sometimes, you walk on the same path again, just to experience your childhood once more.

It was the second time I was travelling on the route from Meerut to Moradabad, but this time, I was with my husband. We were sitting in the back seat and his brother, Neeraj, sat in front with the driver. Tears were still flowing from my eyes. Looking at me, Akhilesh slid a little closer and whispered, 'Stop crying, or we are going back to Meerut. We will stay there until you promise to come with me without tears. I am sure your papa will be happy if we stay with them for a few more days.'

'No, no. I don't want to go back,' I replied, surprisingly.

Neeraj started laughing in the front seat. I realized Akhilesh's whisper was not soft enough. I smiled and stopped crying. Soon, Akhilesh was sleeping, and Neeraj was talking to me. He tried to make me comfortable about the changing environment, telling me about their family and home. He was just in his first year of engineering, and it amazed me to see the maturity level of this 19-year-old boy. His talks assured me that I had a brother in my new home, who would always stand by me. And there was nothing to be afraid of; they were excited to welcome me with affection. I realized that we presume how people would be based on what we see in movies, read in newspapers or watch on news channels. But that's not true of everyone. We should remain positive to explore the good things in life.

We reached Moradabad, and our car stopped at the beginning of a narrow lane. By this time, Akhilesh was wide awake. He said, 'From here, we have to take a short walk. The lane is too narrow for a car to go up to the house.'

Oh yes, this is a really tiny lane, not even a road. Only two-wheelers can enter. I was wearing a sari and heels, and found it difficult to walk, so Akhilesh held my hand.

He whispered in my ear, 'Should I lift you in my arms?'

'No, please, it will be embarrassing,' I replied quickly.

It was a three-storeyed house built in a small area. Everyone welcomed me with excitement. A few rituals at the front door, followed by some games added to the fun. Of course, these allowed me some moments of interaction with Akhilesh's relatives. It was 8 p.m. already, and I hadn't slept well for the past two nights. My sister-in-law Alka brought me some food. I ate a little but I was more exhausted than hungry. As we were having dinner, one of the gas heaters for warmth in the rooms started burning, and huge flames leapt out. Everyone was frightened and began running away, but Akhilesh ran towards the burning flames. He switched it off, but it was still aflame. He then grabbed the burning heater and took it to the open terrace. A few others brought a bucket of water and poured it on the heater. This was my first experience as an army wife. I was scared for Akhilesh when he ran towards the heater. I understood it was the basic instinct of an army person; if they observed any danger, they would run towards it, whereas other people would run away. They think about the safety of others before themselves. That is what they are trained for.

After dinner, Alka took me into a small room that had only two folding beds and a wardrobe. My suitcases were already placed in a corner. She said, 'You can relax here. No one will come here to disturb you. Change your clothes if you like.' I was so tired that I didn't even change my sari. I just made myself comfortable inside the quilt. After a while, I heard a sound as somebody entered my room. 'You are not supposed to sleep alone. It's our first night,' said Akhilesh.

The series of ceremonies had left me feeling so drained that I hadn't even realized it was my 'first night'. Even the room décor didn't remind me, as it was a far cry from the typical 'suhaag raat' setup of Bollywood movies. I got nervous and looked at his smiling face. He had comfortably made space for himself under the same quilt.

'But we hardly know each other,' I whispered.

'We are now husband and wife. And we have a lifetime to get to know each other,' he replied softly.

'I know it's your right, but I'm requesting you to let us be friends first, and allow me the time to fall in love with you. I wanted to have a long courtship with you before marriage, but everything happened so quickly. Please, I am not comfortable yet,' I begged.

He could sense my nervousness. Holding my hand, he said. 'No, this is not about my right. This is about us, our relationship and bonding. I am not at all in a hurry. I know you are mine forever. I don't know how you feel, but I've been in love with you ever since we first met. And now, I see you as my wife.'

I was still uncomfortable.

'Okay, we will be friends first, then lovers, and then, when you agree, we will celebrate our first night traditionally like a newly-married couple.' He hugged me to make me comfortable.

I felt so protected and secure in his arms. Once again, his ideology made me respectful towards him. He was a man I would always admire.

'Can I hug you while sleeping? At least, we can sleep together,' he asked.

I smiled in affirmation and blushed, as I wanted the same. We both hugged each other and slipped inside the quilt. After a while, he said, 'I cannot sleep as your sari has heavy embroidery, and it is poking me. Can you please take it off?'

He was right about my sari, and now it was my turn to accommodate his wishes. I trusted him and knew that he would never let me down. I shyly and hesitantly undraped my sari. He hugged and kissed me, then said, 'Don't worry, I will never break your trust. I love you, and soon you will love me too.'

We both slept well and peacefully. That night I realized the safest place for me on this earth was in the arms of Akhilesh. I was lucky to have such a wonderful person as my life partner. His decency won my heart. Our bond would be built on trust, understanding and affection for each other. Love would definitely happen.

The next day, as is the norm for newly-wed couples, we went to the temple to receive blessings. The pujari gave me the chunari (shawl/stole) of Goddess Durga and said, 'Ma will make you strong and brave. She will protect you from all evils.' At that moment, I didn't know that this blessing would protect me in the future.

On 25 February, we left for our honeymoon to Nainital, a small hill station in north India. Akhilesh had spent six years of his childhood from class six to class 12 at Sainik School Ghorakhal, a place near Nainital. He was attached to his school; it was like his second home. As soon as our car picked up speed, he fell asleep. I noticed car journeys were like a sleeping pill for Akhilesh.

When he woke up, I asked him on a lighter note, 'Why do you sleep every time you sit in a car?'

'An ex-NDA cadet just requires a stable position to sleep. We can sleep anywhere – while sitting, standing or even studying in class, and journeys are the best opportunities. We underwent such rigorous training at the NDA that we were all sleep-deprived, so we caught up on our sleep during journeys, and now it is a habit. You will keep hearing stories of the NDA, as that was the place where I grew from a young boy into an officer.' His explanation further piqued my curiosity about the National Defence Academy.

We reached the Army Holiday Home around 7 p.m. It was bang on the lake just as we entered Nainital. A narrow lane full of beautiful flowers led us to the reception. We moved our luggage into the room – it was a one-bedroom suite with a drawing room, dining area and a small kitchen.

'Have we come here to settle down?' I joked.

'As you wish, Jaaneman. I don't mind. I will settle down anywhere you like,' he replied. 'Let's go for dinner as the mess is open only until 10 p.m. Post that, they will not serve food. They are very particular about the timings. This is the army, not fun (*ye fauj hai, mauj nahin hai*).'

After dinner, we took a walk on the street in front of the reception area. I reached to hold his hand, but to my surprise, he was hesitant to hold mine.

'My soldiers are standing here.'

He maintained a gentle distance between us until we reached the main road. I found him an altogether different person within the army premises; disciplined and firm. An army officer takes special care to maintain the decorum in front of his soldiers, a newly-wed will not break it even on his honeymoon. As soon as we reached the city street, he held my hand gently. It was a long road by the side of the lake, with shops on the other side. A beautiful reflection of lights in the lake and the gentle breeze made the walk romantic. That magical night, we barely noticed anyone except each other. When we reached our room, I savoured his kiss on my lips. The warmth of our bodies was generating heat and we could hear each other's heartbeats. He hugged me and made me feel cosy. I loved the way his arms engulfed me. He was really taking it slow. Sometimes I was naughty, and sometimes, he took a chance. It was like a dream romance, but he kept his promise of waiting until I was ready.

In the morning, we visited his school. There was a small temple on the hill in front of the school gate, and we had to climb a hundred steps to reach it. At the top, thousands of tiny bells were tied all around. People came here to make wishes and tie a bell for every wish. I too tied a bell and made a wish that we would always live together with love. Akhilesh told me he would go to this temple before every exam, when he was a student.

Then we visited the main building of the school. It was a long road from the main gate to the school campus. The landscape was magnificent. At a distance, we could see beautiful snow-covered mountains. The wide-open blue sky was the roof, and the lush-green grounds were the floor, which ended at the white three-storeyed building.

We sat at the edge of the assembly ground, from where we could see the entire valley and the lake at a distance. The breeze kept blowing and carried with it the fragrance of flowers. Akhilesh continued telling me stories, I met the young boy whose ambition it was to become an army officer, a hardworking and sometimes naughty child who created a life for himself by earning scholarships.

Childhood

Akhilesh was eight when the Hindu–Muslim riots took place in his hometown, Moradabad. The entire city was under curfew. The administration ordered people to stay inside their homes. Their house was at the edge of a Muslim colony, so an extra police force had been deployed in that area. The condition worsened, and the Indian Army took charge to restore peace. Little Akhilesh would watch the soldiers standing guard on the streets. Sometimes, it was his duty to offer water, tea and food to the soldiers. Their uniform fascinated him. He sensed how everyone felt secure while the soldiers were around.

'I will be a soldier. I want to wear this uniform and become brave like them,' he told his father.

After a few days, the situation in the city returned to normal. Everyone forgot about the riots and exchanged greetings again. But Akhilesh didn't forget the men who took care of the people during troubled times. He began seeking avenues to join the Indian Army. He had no relatives, friends or even neighbours in the army. Somehow, he found out the address of Sainik School in Ghorakhal and pestered his father to send him there. His father, a humble and warm-hearted person who wished to fulfil his son's desire, got the school's admission form.

'Son, this is a boarding school. The boys have to stay in the hostel. Will you be able to live without us?'

Without hesitation, Akhilesh responded, 'Yes, Papa, I will.'

'You will have to wash your clothes, make your bed and wake up early. Will you be able to manage?' his father asked again.

Akhilesh didn't deviate from his decision. Finally, the condition was if he could get a scholarship, his parents would let him attend the school. Akhilesh passed the entrance exam with a scholarship. His mother didn't want to send her dear son away to boarding school, but she had to give in – his determination was far too strong. So, the budding soldier found a way to fulfil his dreams; he was admitted to class six in Sainik School, Ghorakhal. It was his first step towards joining the Indian Army. He won scholarships throughout his school years, as he was afraid his parents would take him back the year he didn't get a scholarship. With hard work and aspiration, he completed his schooling as the topper of his batch.

Akhlilesh's first attempt at clearing the National Defence Academy (NDA) exam was unsuccessful. His parents were mildly relieved, as they didn't want him joining the army. He then attempted the entrance exam for Delhi College of Engineering at the behest of his parents, and was selected. He joined the college, but his childhood dream of becoming an army officer was still alive.

'I was physically present there, but my heart always wanted to be in the Indian Army. I was not happy,' he recalled. He appeared for the NDA entrance exam once again. This time, he was more focused and determined as his parents warned him it would be his last attempt. 'If you fail this time, accept that you are not born to become an army officer. And then concentrate on your engineering studies,' his mother told him.

'I created my destiny with all the aspirations of my childhood. I made a promise to myself that I would earn this uniform.'

Finally, Akhilesh was selected for the NDA and he approached his parents with the call letter in hand. It was his father who supported him, and said to his mother, 'If he wishes to become an army officer, we should not stand between him and his dreams. Let him go.' His mother appeared unhappy with the decision. 'When I looked at the sad face of my mother, I assured her, "Mummyji, one day, you will be proud of me. Please, let me go." With a heavy heart, she allowed me to join the NDA,' Akhilesh recounted.

'NDA, the place I dreamed of every night. Getting into the academy was tough, but surviving the training and passing out as an officer was the toughest. Total ragra (ragging), rolling, punishment and assemblies was the life we lived 24/7. My best friends are still the ones from the academy, as we survived those days together. The NDA is considered one of the toughest training academies in the world. They make future warriors capable of leading troops to victory across the entire spectrum of conflict. We had varieties of meals displayed in front of us in those days, but we didn't have the time to eat. We slept with open eyes in the theory classes and mastered all the tricks to survive punishment. Those three years made men out of us boys. Now, we can withstand any situation in life with courage. See, I married you.' He laughed and winked at me.

I nodded with a smile and felt like I had known Akhilesh since childhood; like I was present during all his ups and downs, naughty moments and hard-working hours since his school days.

The school bell rang for lunch break. We moved into the building to meet the teachers and principal. Most of the staff appeared new, except for a few old teachers. It was obvious from the warmth of the teachers' smiles that they were delighted to meet Akhilesh. Only a soulful person could have thought of beginning another chapter of his life with the blessings of his teachers. The teachers invited us to have lunch with them in the dining hall. The taste of the rajma-chawal (rice and kidney beans) brought back childhood memories and a smile to Akhilesh's face. After lunch, we visited the hostel rooms of Singh House. Akhilesh's name was written on the board in the list of house captains, at the entrance. We interacted with the students and clicked photographs before returning to Nainital. I could understand why he had taken me there – the school was an integral part of his life, and he had now become an integral part of my life. The sense of belongingness between us was getting stronger. His refreshed childhood memories brought us closer. It was like a bridge between the past and the present.

Later that night, we visited 'Flat', a big flat ground near the lake. It remains decorated and crowded like a fair through the year, with small street vendors selling handmade items from the valley, such as beautiful candles and wooden artefacts. We enjoyed some street food and left with a delicious aftertaste in our mouths. Finally, a bite of ice cream enhanced the chill in the air. The days seemed golden, and the nights felt cosy in each other's arms. Our friendship was growing, and love was bound to follow. We were lucky to have found each other. He was the only person for me, and I became an indispensable part of him.

We had to cut short our trip as Mummyji (my mother-in-law) asked us to return. It's mandatory for a newly-wed couple to be home for the first Holi after marriage. So, on the morning of the 28th, we headed back to Moradabad. On 2 March, the colourful and playful festival of Holi revealed many more naughty stories about Akhilesh. Mummyji said, 'Your groom would throw colour on everyone. So the neighbours and relatives will not spare you now. They've been waiting for you.' Everyone started laughing.

Our room was on the second floor, while the rest of rooms were on the ground floor. Akhilesh took some colour out of a box, which he must have hidden the previous night. While applying pink gulal on my cheeks, he said, 'Love you, I can't miss playing Holi with you.' And he rubbed my cheeks to his. Then, as instructed by Mummyji, Akhilesh locked me inside and went downstairs. For me, it was time to sleep. Yes, I missed all the fun that was going on downstairs. Around 2 p.m., Mummyji brought me food. She had prepared everything herself just to keep me safe. I felt blessed even though she always kept her distance and never hugged me. I knew she was a loving mother at heart. The qualities of her professional life were reflected at home – a strict, disciplinarian mother. I admired how she had dedicated her life to her children's studies and their futures.

We continued our honeymoon after the Holi festival. This time, we travelled to Jim Corbett National Park. The resort had aesthetic glimpses of an old village, with husked roofs and lamps hanging at the doors. There were fields at the side of the resort. A narrow pathway through the middle of the fields led to the river behind the village. The sight of elephants by the roadside was normal, as people kept them as pets and used them as a mode of transport. The smells of wet soil, wood and wild animals were all around in the air. We clocked extra miles of our relationship in that beautiful, wild ambience. Luckily, we both prefer lush green and dense forests to the illumination of big cities. Holding each other's hands, we would walk the path between the fields to reach the river, then cross the river and sit on the rocks in the middle. The sound of the flowing water and the sight of the low mountains was mesmerizing. In every walk with nature, we received far more than we sought. We adopted the pace of nature: her secret is patience. With patience, we embarked on the journey of love. I would shave him, give him massages and brush his teeth, and he would walk carrying me on his back, feed me and give me massages too. I met the man of my dreams just like Sleeping Beauty or Ariel the mermaid did. The moments of love were slowly melting the two of us. Our breath was now filled with the fragrance of our bodies. He never forced his desire on me, but we explored the intimacy and depth of our relationship like lovers.

After three days, we returned home. He had to resume duty soon, and Mummyji wanted to teach me their religious customs, so we stayed at home for a week. It was compulsory for me to wear sindoor, red bindi, bangles, toe rings, earrings, a gold chain and my engagement ring. Traditionally, these are all signs of a Hindu married woman. It is considered unlucky for husbands if their wives miss wearing any of them. My mother-in-law was somewhat liberal, so she permitted me to wear Indian suits instead of saris the entire day. But I had to cover my head in front of everyone. This was the tradition in every house in Moradabad. All the religious rituals like fasting and so on were the responsibilities of the women. Mummyji herself was wholly devoted to all the social norms, so her expectations of me were the same. I respected her feelings and tried my best to adopt her ways. I did whatever she asked me, just to satisfy her. But the reality was different when I was growing up. Even though my paternal grandparents lived with us, I never saw my mother do the same things as Mummyji. Ma followed the Arya Samaj way and offered prayers to God daily, but no other rituals were needed. She just believed in having faith in God and karma (good deeds); I was the same as my Ma.

A LADY IN THE ARMY REGIMENT

The few days I spend with you are worth the thousands of days I spend without you.

No road is long if you travel with your companion. Akhilesh and I drove around 600 km from Moradabad to Firozpur, to the regiment where he was posted. It was a small town in Punjab, also known as the land of martyrs. Three heroic martyrs of India who were killed for raising their voices against the British – Shaheed Bhagat Singh, Rajguru and Sukhdev – have their final resting places on the banks of the Sutlej River in Firozpur. Its cantonment is the army base for the Hussainiwala Border post, the international border between India and Pakistan. The entire journey was like a tutorial class for me, transitioning from civilian society to the defence world, as Akhilesh briefed me about army and regiment life. He wanted me to fit into his world perfectly. And a pride-filled smile didn't leave his handsome face for even a second, as he spoke.

'I belong to Indian Artillery or "The God of War". We are the bearers of massive guns, have vision from far behind the target, and can impact from a distance of 40 km. The supporters of infantry and the actual conquerors of the war. It is said that "Artillery conquers, and infantry occupies". A toast to the guns – by them we live, for without them, we would die. Whatever the mission, we'll give it a try.

We'll serve them with honour, for they are the ones that make us "gunners".'

They seemed to be his favourite lines, as he had memorized them. I could sense the passion this army officer had for his work. It was as though he was deeply in love with his guns.

Artillery regiments can be Light, Medium, Field, Missile, Rocket or SATA (Surveillance & Target Acquisition) based on the guns they possess. Capt. Akhilesh was commissioned as a lieutenant in the 223 Medium regiment. They call themselves 'The Silencers' because 'When we fight, everyone else goes quiet.' The regiment is like the family of a soldier that stays together through thick and thin. They live, learn and die fighting with the enemy, together. 'Raising Day' is when a regiment/battalion/unit/paltan is formed in the Indian Army. Every regiment maintains records of the history of battles fought, weapons, gallantry awards and more. This family treats its CO as a father figure, who is often nicknamed 'Tiger'. His orders and decisions are final, no one questions them. The performance of the regiment depends on the personality and leadership qualities of its CO. Soldiers of the regiment are divided into four batteries. As Battery Commanders, officers lead their batteries for war, and keep them fit and ready to fight. They attend the administrative office every morning. In the afternoon, they may go home for lunch. Evenings are reserved for physical exercises and sports. They have their training sessions on campus and sometimes, travel to remote areas as well. A soldier can give up his life for the izzat (honour) of his paltan.

The ladies of the regiment have a unique role to play. They support their regiment by taking care of each other and their families. Their husbands may be posted to remote areas, but these ladies never lose contact with each other. They are all part of the Army Wives Welfare Association (AWWA). It is a voluntary, self-help organization dedicated to the welfare of soldiers' families. The army officer's wives manage most of the activities of this association.

Akhilesh said, 'You will enjoy the welfare activities. Officers' wives of our unit teach useful and creative skills to the soldier's wives.'

I inquired, 'What kind of creative work?'

'Painting, dancing, tailoring, clay work, embroidery, makeup, cooking and more. They equip them with skills to help them make a living if ever required,' he elaborated. 'But for you, my CO has something else in mind,' he added with a mischievous grin.

'What do you mean?'

'We faujis (army folk) know how to use our resources. You've quit your job but don't worry, the regiment will keep you busy.' His smile lit up his eyes.

'How?'

'You will conduct computer training classes for the officers of the unit. This is my CO's decision. He has tried everything to get the officers to learn how to operate computers, but all his tricks have failed. Officers behave like gentlemen in front of ladies. Now, the responsibility lies on your shoulders.'

'What tricks?'

'First, the CO tried to tie our leaves with the computer assignments, but it didn't work. Then, he sent one of the bright soldiers from our unit, Mangeram, to Delhi to learn how to use computers. My CO himself is a learned man who believes computers will become a necessity in the coming years. He ordered Mangeram to conduct classes for the officers, but he could not maintain discipline in the class as a junior soldier. Senior officers keep asking questions like "Why is this called a mouse? Why can't we call it a cat?" Poor Mangeram, he was always so confused. The fact is officers are not willing to learn how to use computers.'

'Oh! But why?' I asked

'We find it difficult. We can handle guns, run for miles and carry out the most daring operations, but computers... it's boring!' Akhilesh replied.

Then, he asked, 'Do you know how to sing?'

'I sing for my pleasure. I am not a trained singer. Why do you ask?'

'It is tradition in our regiment for a newly-wed couple to sing a duet at the "dining-in",' he explained.

'What is a dining-in?'

'It is a party thrown for new members. This time it will be for you. They had one for me too when I was first commissioned here. All regiments have a unique way of welcoming new members, and it is different for officers joining and a new bride coming in.'

'How do they welcome officers?' I was curious.

'So, commissioned officers are welcomed twice; first, with just the officers of the unit. That's the "wining-in". Next, they are welcomed at the dining-in with the ladies present too.' He explained, 'Wining-in is an informal army tradition to check the drinking potential of a new officer and welcome him into the regiment. He has to finish a goblet full of liquor; a cocktail of every available brand in the mess, in three gulps. After each gulp, he must wipe his moustache – whether he has one or not – and say, "I drink for the izzat of my paltan". If he makes a mistake or fails at any stage, this drill is repeated the next day.'

'Oh my God, it must be difficult.' My eyes widened in surprise.

'Yes, it is, especially for teetotallers.' He nodded.

'How did you do manage?'

'I was a teetotaller and fainted in the middle of the drill, so I had to repeat it,' he said, adding, 'The next day, the Havaldar Sahab of my battery gave me a lot of butter to eat. He said, "*Sahab aap ko paltan ki izzat rakhni hai. Aaj aapko nahin girna hai. Ye khalo, aapko kuchh nahin hoga.* (Sir, you need to preserve the honour of our battery. You mustn't faint and fall today. Eat this and nothing will happen to you.)".'

'So, did you complete the drill the following day?'

'Yes, I did,' he replied with pride. 'And my other saviours were my immediate seniors. They have guided me with all the traditions of the regiment and saved me every time from the CO whenever I committed any blunders. Major J.S. Cheema, Major Sanjay Kahol and Captain Manish Marwaha were like guiding angels to me.'

'Okay, so you share a good bond with them.'

'It's a life-long bond, dear. Although they've been transferred from my regiment now, you will keep hearing their stories from me.'

I just smiled at him, observing his gratitude towards his seniors.

'And how do they welcome ladies?' I asked.

'Sometimes, they cook up false stories about officers to scare the new bride. You must not believe them. I have a clean past and I haven't done anything questionable. Except for cooking up many stories and scaring newcomers,' he said, laughing out loud.

'Oh! They will take their revenge on me.'

'Definitely, but I am too good. No one else has that talent.' He was confident that it would not be that effective this time, as he would not be part of the mischief-makers.

'Okay then, I should focus on the song. Which song should we practise?' I asked him.

'Any duet that has the minimum male portion, as I sing terribly,' he laughed again.

We decided to sing *'Jaane ja... dhoondta phir raha hoon.'* So, all he had to sing was *'Main yahaan... '*

Soon, we were on a long, narrow road flanked by green crop fields. We could spot tiny, yellow mustard flowers for miles, which made the landscape sublime. This was the majestic land of Punjab. We stopped to freshen up, before entering the cantonment area of Firozpur. I straightened the pleats of my light blue sari and he changed his shirt. I was about to introduce myself to a world I had only dreamed of until then. When we arrived, all the officers of the 223 Medium regiment, and their families, were standing outside the officers' mess. The CO, Col V.K. Singh, his wife and all the other officers' wives received us with great warmth. Major V.S. Mathai, Major Shakti Jaitley, Major Sudarshan, Captain S.S. Sidhu, Captain Vishal Sharma and Lieutenant Rajesh Das were all excitedly waiting to pull Capt. Akhilesh's leg. They made him sit on a horse and took him around the cantonment accompanied by band-baaja (live music) in the middle of the afternoon, while I stood with the other ladies of the unit near the officer's mess. Since they hadn't attended our wedding, they made us repeat the jaimala. It was such fun, and I felt an instant connection to each and every member of The Silencers.

That night, I stayed in Akhilesh's bachelor room to fulfil the wishes of his juniors. It was the first room in the row of the single officers' mess, as he was the senior-most among the youngsters.

'We've left the room exactly as sir kept it. We wanted you to witness it for yourself,' Capt. Vishal said, grinning wickedly.

I peeked inside. It was a big room with all the furniture dragged toward a corner, near a wooden cabinet. The cabinet was empty, except for two olive uniforms hanging neatly inside. A heap of clothes was lying on the side, hiding what appeared to be a single-seater sofa touching one side of the single bed. There was a table on the other side of the bed. I saw unorganized books, mugs, shaving cream, aftershave lotion, shoe polish, toothpaste and even a toothbrush on it. There were many pairs of shoes under the bed. In contrast, the other corner of the room was neatly arranged, with a large television. And a sizeable portion of the room was empty.

'Sir bought the TV recently. That's why that corner is so neat,' Capt. Vishal said.

'It looks shabby to you because you are from a civilian background,' Akhilesh said immediately.

I looked at him for an explanation.

'See, in the army, we deal with emergencies. We are always in hurry, there is no time to open cabinets. I kept everything within my reach from the bed so I wouldn't be late for duty. It's necessary in the army,' Akhilesh explained with a straight face.

'Oh!' I assumed it to be true, while his juniors giggled outside the room.

The next day, we moved into the guest house. The dining-in party to welcome me into the regiment had been organized in the officer's mess that evening. As requested by everyone, I wore my wedding outfit. All the ladies were dressed in Indian formal wear, mainly saris. The entrance looked heavenly, decorated with tiny lights and vibrant plants. As a mark of respect, everyone had to be present five minutes before the CO and his wife arrived. The seating arrangement on the lawn was meant only for the ladies, and it was done according to the ranks of their husbands. I was next to the CO's wife since the party was for me. Suddenly, I had to recognize myself as Mrs Saxena because it was the name by which everyone addressed me. It was awkward for me to keep sitting as senior officers approached to greet me. I was instructed not to stand even for higher-ranking officers, as women in the army are shown respect above all ranks. After a bit of interaction, to my surprise I was made to stand on top of the centre table and sing. But I sang the duet alone because Akhilesh forgot to sing his part! When I reached the end of the song, he shouted from the back, '*Main yahaan, Main yahaan, Main yahaan...* (I am here, I am here, I am here...)' And everyone burst out laughing.

It was also the first time I had seen an alcoholic drink in Akhilesh's hands, and I could not stop my tears. Various thoughts were running through my mind. *Oh my God! I have a sharaabi* (drunkard) *husband. What will I do now?'* My impressions about drinking alcohol had not been good until then.

Akhilesh saw me and murmured, 'Oh my God! Why is she crying? She must be feeling homesick.'

He quickly came up to me and inquired, 'What happened? Are you missing your mom?'

I nodded because I just wanted to leave early. He then pleaded, 'Please don't cry now, the CO will think I've made you cry, and he will punish me. Please, just hold back your tears until he leaves.'

Suddenly, I realized the power of being an army wife. 'Stop drinking,' I said firmly.

He then figured out why I was crying. 'Oh! I see! Well, I can't leave this drink now. In the army, we drink in honour of the CO and our regiment. He will feel offended,' he said, tricking me again into saving his peg. To convince me and avoid any further drama, he added, 'One drink is compulsory in the army. Let me finish this and I will not pour myself another drink.'

It took me a few weeks to understand the cultural differences between civilian life and being in the army. As far as my experience went, at civilian parties or wedding receptions, alcohol was served under the table. Most people lost their senses and sometimes even misbehaved after drinking. But in the army, officers drank openly and always behaved like gentlemen. If an officer was observed to be out of line, there was sure to be disciplinary action against him the next morning.

Cantonment mornings begin much before the first ray of the sun; there is no excuse for last night's pegs. Soldiers are on the running tracks with the officers leading from the front. During drills, the sound of their direct moulded sole (DMS) boots can easily be heard in the balconies. Akhilesh took me around to show me the regiment. At the gate, there was a symbol with the line: *Sarvatra Izzat O Iqbal* (Everywhere with honour and glory). It's the motto of the Indian Artillery. They believe they win whenever artillery guns are fired. The guard opened the gate. A well-maintained, vast area with a lot of greenery was before me. The pathway soil was brick-red in colour, white-coloured bricks marked both the edges of the path, and the buildings were yellow. The combination of the three colours enhanced the entire place. To the left of the gate, I noticed a structure I had never seen earlier in my life. It was a building with symbols of all the religions of India together on the wall. Inside, to my surprise, representations of various gods of all religions were placed on one platform under the same roof. This unique and fascinating structure is called the Sarv Dharm Sthal.

'This is not unique to our regiment. It is a common feature in every regiment of the Indian Army. At any religious ceremony, whether Hindu, Sikh, Muslim or Christian, the CO or Subedar Major performs the regimental havan, and people of all faiths come together in devotion under a common roof at the Sarv Dharm Sthal,' Akhilesh explained.

Such a wonderful tradition that weaves the untearable fabric of the Indian Army, with the acceptance of all religions and beliefs. It was then that my heart accepted the Indian Army as the most magnificent organization on earth.

After a short while of sitting in devotion at Sarv Dharm Sthal, Akhilesh took me around to see the regiment's batteries. The soldiers and the officers of the artillery regiment are divided into four batteries; Papa, Cubic, Romeo and Headquarter. The first three batteries handle the maintenance and execution of six big guns, which require at least 10 soldiers to fire a shell/missile. The last battery, Headquarter, takes care of administration. Next, we went to see the office but I didn't enter, as it was in operation. I left Akhilesh there and returned to the guest room with an even deeper admiration for the army.

We moved into married accommodation within a week. The house was adjacent to the main road, and we had a small quarter on the first floor, above Capt. Sidhu and his family. I saw some hens and a dog in their garden. I thought, *Amazing! They are fond of pets.* Until the next morning, when our doorbell was rung. A soldier stood in front of me with a small box filled with vegetables, eggs and bread, placed on the ground, and a rooster in his hand.

'What is all this?' I asked.

'Memsahib, *aapka ration hai* (these are your groceries/ food rations). It is all fresh,' he replied, and then asked, 'Where should I put it?' He pointed to the rooster and the box.

'No, no, I am a vegetarian. Please take this rooster away!' I told him without wasting a minute.

'Oh! Memsahib, *list mei toh non-veg likha hai* (but your name is in the list of non-vegetarians).' He was confused.

'It must be a mistake. Please change it,' I said. From that moment, I turned into a 'vegetarian' as I could not handle the 'fresh' rations of the fauj! I realized then why Capt. Sidhu was fond of 'pets'.

For at least half an hour in the evening, Akhilesh and I both laughed holding our stomachs when I narrated the incident. He listed our names intentionally as he was aware of the consequences. He just wanted to see what lengths I would go to for chicken, one of my favourite foods. 'Oh my God! You are such a fraud,' I said while still holding my tummy, which was aching after laughing so hard.

I started unpacking our luggage and decorating our home. Many of our wedding gifts remained untouched because we never had the opportunity to open them together, as we had promised to do earlier. He was busy at the office in the mornings, evenings were for exercise drills and later, we would be at some officer's house. This is another tradition of the regiment; the married officers take turns inviting the newly-weds for dinner. This allows a new bride the opportunity to adapt to her new environment and settle down smoothly. The wives of other officers guide and support the new entrant. We always carried a gift for the host family, as part of army culture. Every home displayed a reflection of India. You could find corners decorated with handicrafts from different regions of India: Rajasthan, Nagaland, Assam, Kashmir and so on. They lived a nomadic life and collected local artefacts from their various postings. These homes didn't have luxuries and expensive items, but I found them to be the most beautiful, creative and cosy spaces.

On 4 April, I waited for the stroke of midnight and the date to change. I pulled out a few gifts, which I had wrapped earlier, from my wardrobe, and woke Akhilesh with a kiss. 'Happy birthday, Hubby,' I whispered in his ear.

He wrapped me in his arms and kissed me. 'You are the best thing that has happened to me,' he said lovingly.

'Let's go for a ride. I want your first birthday with me to be memorable.' I pulled him out of bed. He was equally excited and soon, we were riding the cantonment roads on his motorbike.

We were out until dawn; he showed me every park and crossroad in the area.

In the morning, I headed towards the market as soon as Akhilesh left for work. My husband's buddy (helper), Hassan Bhaiyya, insisted on coming along so I would not get lost in the city. I found out later that he had instructions not to leave me alone if I was stepping out. He was in charge of Akhilesh's uniforms – what he needed to wear to the office or for sports in the evening, which belts and shoes were to be paired with them – he knew it all better than I did. He always kept the stars that Capt. Akhilesh wore on his shoulders and cap shining. He was like Aladdin's genie; he would appear whenever his officer required him.

Monday was usually a long day. Akhilesh returned in the evening. He rang the doorbell, but no one opened the door. After ringing the bell a few times, he realized the door was open. He pushed the door and entered the drawing room. His eyes sparkled as he discovered the floor filled with balloons and candles. I entered the room with a cake on a platter. His face radiated with affection and gratitude. He kissed my forehead, and said, 'You are a blessing for me. I left home as a child, and all these years later, I feel like I've returned home. You've become the reason for my happiness. I love you more than you will ever understand, Shikha.'

I blushed and said, 'I understand. Now go inside and change your clothes. I have a new shirt for you. And I've also prepared some snacks, eat them before they turn cold.'

He realized I had spent the entire day preparing for his birthday celebration. 'Today, I will take you out for dinner. Don't cook anything,' he announced.

After cutting the cake, we went out for dinner but there wasn't a single elegant restaurant in Firozpur. We managed somehow and then decided that the officer's mess was the best place to dine out.

One afternoon, Akhilesh was sleeping so peacefully that I didn't want to disturb him. I wasn't aware that in the army, sports have a special status. You don't just play for fitness, but to stay connected with the men you command and to remind them that winning is precious. It brings a sense of glory.

His buddy came running to the front door, and asked, '*Sahab kahan hai.* (Where is sir?)'

'Sleeping,' I calmly replied.

'*Utha do* (Wake him up).' I was surprised that Hassan would want to interrupt his officer's sleep. I woke Akhilesh up.

'Oh! Shit! I am late for the drill,' Akhilesh said, rushing to get ready.

A couple of hours later, I approached the front door when the bell rang.

'I hope you slept well. Did the medicine work?' Akhilesh raised his hand to touch my forehead, while entering the house. The CO and his wife were behind him, as he had told them I was unwell. I didn't know what to say or how to react. I remained quiet with a blank expression on my face.

The two of them left shortly, so I could get some rest.

'At least inform me beforehand when I am sick,' I said in an amused tone.

'You didn't wake me up, so you have to cover for me. I didn't expect them to come home with me, but you managed well.' He smiled and put his arms around my waist.

In the regiment, bachelors are mostly juniors who stay and eat at the officer's mess. And they have the right to knock on any married officer's door asking for food. Since they live alone, they were always welcomed into the families. I spent a lot of time with the bachelors. They often appeared at dinner time for scrambled eggs and parathas. They would help me in the kitchen, as Akhilesh had jokingly told them I was terrible at cooking. Any kind of food was appreciated on the table. The aim was to have fun. Akhilesh's course-mates, Captain Raj Narayan Tiwari, Captain Rakesh Ranjan and Captain Anuranjan Srivastava were also posted at the same cantonment. They became like my family members.

Akhilesh's commitment to his duties in the mornings and evenings meant that we could barely spend time together, just the two of us. Moreover, friends and juniors were always hanging around after work hours. One evening, Akhilesh put a lock on the front door and jumped from the terrace on to our veranda, to get inside the house. He wanted us to be alone for a while. The doorbell rang just as he held me in his arms and began kissing me passionately.

'*Saale, bahar aaja* (Dude, come out). I know you are inside,' shouted Capt. Tiwari.

'*Saale, chala ja* (Dude, go away),' Akhilesh yelled from inside and added softly, 'Spare me some time with my wife.'

'I've come to invite you both for dinner tomorrow,' Capt. Tiwari shouted again.

'Okay, we will come tomorrow. But right now, I will not open the door,' Akhilesh yelled back.

That was the height of the informal relationships I witnessed between course-mates. One came over with an invitation, and the other refused to open the door but accepted the invitation! The next evening, we were at Capt. Tiwari's regiment officers' mess for dinner and he gifted me a beautiful jewellery box that still contains my precious ornaments. Their friendship was like an unshakeable bond.

One day, we all went to a beautiful, big lake near Hussainiwala checkpost for a picnic. Around sunset, the silence at Hussainiwala Border was ruptured by thunderclaps of the heavy boots of Indian Border Security Force (BSF) Jawans and Pakistani Rangers. Both sides were well-dressed in their ceremonial uniforms. Indian BSF Jawans in khaki and Pakistani Rangers in long, black kurta-pyjamas. Both teams matched their steps, movement and motions with each other, under the loud commands of their commanders, for the retreat ceremony of de-hoisting the national flags of both countries, with full honours. The sound of the patriotic songs evoked a sense of national pride among the audience on both sides of the border, leaving an indelible mark in my memory. The endless applause in praise of their movements boosted the morale of the guards, fuelling them with energy. Until 1970, there was no retreat ceremony at this check post. Then one fine day, Inspector General, BSF, Ashwani Kumar Sharma, called upon authorities from both countries to have a joint parade. Since then, it has become a tradition.

In just a couple of weeks, I had transformed into an army person. These people are above religion; humanity and brotherhood are the basis of their living. It's one big family; with due respect given to rank and seniority, everyone has their place, identity and responsibility. Still, they are all painted in one colour – olive green. Patriotism is the foundation of their every action, tradition and custom. They're always willing to sacrifice their lives for the nation. I was so proud to be associated with the Indian Army. It was like being in a completely different world. The cantonment, filled with patriotic and inspiring slogans, provides an inspiring environment for everyone to develop patriotism as the fundamental character of their personality. Love for the tricolour was in the air; we breathed it every moment. And it reminded us to live with honour. Slogans such as 'Serve your country' or 'Nation First' even inspire children to build patriotic character. It left me with just one thought: Why can't my entire country adopt an environment like this?

POSTING TO KASHMIR

Only the strongest woman can survive with
half of her heart missing.

I was sitting on the back seat of a Jonga, a rugged army vehicle built of heavy iron. If you touched the bonnet in the summer, you could get blisters. All the officers with their families were travelling to Jalandhar to attend a social engagement at the division headquarters. I had also planned to shop for curtains and sofa upholstery, as the options for home furnishings were limited in Firozpur.

With the officers busy in meetings through the day, the ladies planned food menus, table layouts and decorated the lawn. We were also rehearsing a qawwali (a form of Sufi devotional singing), for 'Husband's Night'. Another a beautiful tradition of the army, Husband's Night is a thanksgiving party organized by the women, for all the officers of the division.

The Indian Army also shows immense respect towards women in many of its gestures and traditions. Food is first served to ladies, and even the most senior officer will begin his meal after them. And a lady is always addressed as 'Ma'am.'

The large, open lawn had been decorated with tiny, sparkling lights. The stage was on one side, with neatly laid-out white chairs on the other side. There was soft music playing in the background, and I was looking for Akhilesh who hadn't arrived yet. It was my turn to go on stage for the qawwali, and I still couldn't spot him. Finally, I noticed him at the back, behind the chairs. He looked at me; I smiled and received a smile in return, but the spark in his smile was missing. Soon after the stage shows, everyone was on the dance floor. I went to get Akhilesh to join in, but he was reluctant.

'What's wrong? Are you okay?'

'Yes, I am good.' But his answer was not in sync with his expression.

'He got an SOS (Save Our Souls) posting order today. Soon, he has to join the 1889 Light Regiment at Tangmarg, Kashmir,' Col V.K. Singh told me, while placing his hand on the shoulder of his dear officer. 'I will miss him, as he one of the most dazzling officers of my regiment,' he added with pride.

I was shocked, and then I realized the reason behind Akhilesh's silence.

'When do we have to go to Kashmir?' I asked.

His CO replied again 'Not you, he will go alone, within a month. It is a field station, families are not allowed.'

This was depressing news. We knew we would have to live without each other sometimes, but we had just gotten married. My mind could not accept this news that came like a surprise punch. Suddenly, someone from the back commented, 'This is destiny; it changes after marriage. Even Ram had to go to vanvasa (exile) after his marriage. Sita brought that misfortune upon him.'

Hearing that, my tears started dropping. *How could anybody think like this? When Ram went to vanvasa, how was it Sita's fault?* It was first time in my life that I'd heard Goddess Sita being associated with bad luck. This comment hurt me deeply. I didn't want to be tagged as the bringer of misfortune to my husband.

'Oh! No! Please don't cry.' Akhilesh reacted quickly. 'You are my strength. I believe Ram became a god only because of his vanvasa and Goddess Sita.' He tried to cheer me up by saying, 'They allow families in the summer. I will get you there.'

Then he pulled me to the dance floor. 'Let's dance.'

It was difficult for me, but I tried. We were both sad but kept smiling and dancing just to cheer each other up.

Remote postings and separations are part of army life. All the officers and their wives have faced this kind of a situation at some point in their lives. I knew that the role of an army wife was challenging. I was prepared for the separation, just not so early on in our marriage. It had been just a few weeks since I'd accompanied my husband to Firozpur, and now I would have to return. '*Where would I go? To my parents' or my in-laws' place? What about our home? When would we be together again?*' With all these questions up in the air, the posting to Kashmir remained a bitter fact that I had to face.

We returned home in an unpleasant mood. Now, I had to repack everything. Around 5 a.m. the next day, regiment trucks and jeeps approached the Rajasthan desert. All the officers and soldiers left for a 15-day-long pre-planned training session. Akhilesh joined them as he hadn't yet received his official posting orders; we expected the orders to arrive within a month. I was alone at home when Capt. Sidhu's daughter came over.

'Ma has sent me to call you. Come and have lunch with us, as you are alone.' Her gesture touched my heart.

She was just a teenager but she'd witnessed army life since birth. When I went downstairs, Capt. Sidhu's wife greeted me with empathy and offered me a seat next to her at the table. I had a pleasant lunch and was able to eat well only because I was with them.

'We've seen these empty fields and roads several times before. But at least we know they will return. You take care though, Kashmir is not a good posting,' Mrs Sidhu said with concern.

'I understand, but duty is duty,' I paused and replied while sipping a glass of water.

'I can't say how far this is true, but I've heard gossip that something is not right in the Valley.'

I looked at her with a question on my face. She looked back, worried. There was just silence for a few minutes, until her daughter finally said, '*Papaji kehte hain, jaake rakho saiyan maar sake na koi* (When God protects you, no harm can come to you).'

'Yes, true. Why should we worry? It's just a posting, and we are imagining the worst,' Mrs Sidhu said, perhaps in an attempt to comfort me. We ignored the worries in our minds for a while and tried to smile.

Around 7 p.m., I arrived at the CO's house, as Hassan had earlier passed on a dinner invitation to me from the family. 'Please sit. Shikha, I hope you are okay,' Mrs Singh said as we sat down on the sofa. 'Please come and stay with me until the officers return from training. We have a guest room. This must be your first time alone.'

'Yes, I've never stayed alone before. But I am fine. I will soon get used to this.'

'Yes, that's true. Over time, we learn how to live by ourselves and manage everything... children's education, caring for aged parents and so on. We stay strong so our husbands can concentrate on their duties. Their jobs are tough, working with weapons and ammunition. Even a tiny mistake could prove to be dangerous. We have to keep them calm and free from additional worries, so we handle all the domestic nuisances and troubles by ourselves.' She counselled me, speaking from her own experience.

Mrs Singh, her kids and I had dinner together. Earlier, the kids were busy playing or studying. They seemed familiar and comfortable with their father's absence. During dinner, Mrs Singh shared her experiences in the army. She said, 'You must accompany your husband on his postings as far as possible. Don't fear the forests, hills or even the desert. I've lived in a place where I sometimes found snakes on the floor, as I stepped out of bed. In some locations, you will have just a tent to live in, and often have to deal with water shortage or do without electricity. Yet, you mustn't miss the opportunity to live with your husband whenever possible. Or else, most of your married life will be spent apart.'

Then, I asked her about the disturbance in the Valley. She replied affirmatively and said there was robust information in the regiment about an uneasy situation in the Valley. It was highly probable that some regiments deployed in Kashmir could receive orders to move towards the LOC. It was a perplexing situation; no one knew exactly what was happening at the border.

The following day, all the ladies of the regiment got together for an AWWA meeting. It was an official meeting with strict protocols being followed. This was where I learnt that women are the lifeline of the organization. The welfare of the soldiers is an officer's responsibility, and the responsibility of the soldiers' families lies with the officer's wife. They're there for each other under every imaginable circumstance. Sometimes, the soldiers are not even aware of how the women tackle challenges. When Malawati was pregnant, the ladies of the unit looked after her just like family. They accompanied her on medical check-ups, and supported her in completing household chores while her husband was busy with his duties. They even made clothes for the new-born. When Sipahi Puran's Singh son fell from the terrace of his house and broke his leg, the officers' wives took him to the hospital. The boy was walking when the soldier returned home. When the daughter of a soldier, Ramlal Yadav, needed advice with regard to her higher studies, the officers' wives guided her. When Mrs Basu was about to deliver her first child, instead of her husband, his course-mate and his wife waited outside the operation theatre in the middle of the night. Soni preferred living in the separated family (SF) quarters of the army cantonment when her husband was posted to the field area, as she was afraid of staying at her in-laws' place in the village. She was once molested by her husband's uncle in a drunken state. When Colonel Verma got a remote posting, Mrs Verma lived at SF with her son, so the boy could complete his school session, being in class 10. Her friends in the army became her support system. Officers' wives guided the widow of gunner Kishanlal after his death, when a property dispute disrupted their joint family in the village, and she was left with three kids and no money. Several such stories reflect the brotherhood in arms managed smoothly and silently by the women of the organization. We were like extended families to each other; a sense of belonging guided each of us. And the beauty of this relationship is that you remain connected for life, within or outside the organization, even after the death of an army man. I had never observed such strong bonds anywhere else.

Officers' wives help decorate the officers' mess, with their ingenuity and admirable shopping skills. They are also partly involved in managing the regiment's social events. Most officer's wives are well-educated, postgraduate professionals often choosing to live with their husbands in remote locations around the country. However, when these 'nomads' get opportunities to live in cities, they take advantage of their educational and professional qualifications to work in firms or at schools. I was in awe of the fact that I'd become part of such a strong and brave fraternity, which was deeply affectionate as well. If soldiers are the mind of the army, the women are its heart. Their thought processes are reflected in their children's upbringing and home environments. They understand loneliness and are willing to share, care, support and guide each other. While men are trained to fight for the country, women gear themselves up to deal with all the stress and responsibilities. It is true that God chose the strongest ladies and paired them with soldiers. Ladies make sure that beauty, peace and harmony permeate the environment of the cantonment. Without the support of women, this establishment will lose its warmth. Both men and women contribute equally to the pride and dignity of our nation.

The third day after the officers had left for training was a hot Sunday afternoon. All the kids were playing at our house as it was largely empty; I had packed up most of the stuff. I was in the kitchen, cooking pulao for the children, when the sound of DMS boots in the drawing room alerted me. I popped out and found Akhilesh standing in his summer combat uniform. I was pleasantly surprised.

'How come you've returned so early?'

'I was missing you, so I've come back to see you.' He smiled.

'Really?' I asked suspiciously.

He looked at the kids, ignored my question, and said, 'I am hungry. Is the food ready?'

'Sure, I'll serve lunch.'

During lunch, he was silent as opposed to his usual talkative self, but the kids had a good time. Soon, all of them returned to their homes. While clearing the dining table, I asked Akhilesh, 'What's happened?'

'I have to report to the 1889 Light Regiment in Tangmarg, Kashmir, within four days. My CO received this message from the headquarters yesterday. So, all the officers and soldiers gave me a farewell at the training camp. We will have to leave tomorrow. I hope you've packed everything.' His voice was solemn as he spoke.

'Oh, so early! There seems to be an emergency. Is everything okay in Kashmir?' I asked worriedly.

'There is no news of any emergency. It is just the usual procedure. It happens sometimes.' He tried convincing me but I could see his words lacked conviction.

Mrs Singh, along with all the other officers' wives, hosted a dine-out for us. The following day, we left Firozpur with our fauji trunks, and headed towards Moradabad. As Gurudwara Paonta Sahib was on the way, we took blessings from the divine guru. It is a beautiful holy place built with white marble on the banks of the river Yamuna.

The sudden change had created some turbulence in my mind. When situations are not under our control, we tend to turn to the Almighty. We took a night halt at my parent's place in Dehradun, which was just two hours away. When we arrived at Moradabad the next evening, our luggage had already been dropped off. Hassan, and another soldier, Ratan, placed 10 fauji trunks on the second floor at my in-laws' house. As I prepared tea for everyone, there was silence in the veranda next to the kitchen. I found the ground floor empty so I took the tea to the terrace of the second floor. I could hear Mummyji and Akhilesh talking, but they stopped as soon as I entered. They sipped their tea in silence, and I could sense the tension in the air. At night, I asked him about the conversation.

'Shikha, people make mountains out of mole hills. One of her close friends believes you did not follow the proper customs during our wedding, which is why we are at this stage so early in our married life. Mummy is just worried about us.' He answered without looking towards me.

'Really! But isn't this a regular part of army life? I've met many ladies in the regiment who've undergone this kind of separation.' I felt wretched.

'I know it's a regular thing in the army, but this small town has never experienced this.' He sounded disappointed too.

'Which custom did I not follow?'

'During the pheras, you were supposed to wear a yellow sari but you didn't. You were in the same lehenga you wore during the jaimala,' Akhilesh said.

'But no one told me it was necessary to wear a yellow sari. Or else, I would have worn it. Do you also think that my wedding lehenga is the reason for your posting?'

'Ridiculous, this is insane, I would never think that. It could never be the reason for our separation.'

It was the second time I had been blamed for Capt. Akhilesh's posting to Kashmir, and I could not hold back the tears. I was sad and hurt. Akhilesh wrapped his arms around me, and said, 'If you weep this way, how will I be able to leave you behind? Become my strength so I may leave with a calm mind. Be strong and let no one disrupt your faith. Do you think you are the reason for my posting?'

'No, not at all.' I was firm.

'I believe the same, so stay positive. And always remember, I will be fine if you are smiling. So keep smiling always.' He kissed me gently, and then said, 'It would be nice if you resumed working at your computer education centre in Dehradun. You will be busy, and I will be at ease. I have called Papa from Dehradun to take you. He will come tomorrow.'

I was not strong enough to handle all these changes. My tears just wouldn't stop. He was feeling low too. We were both sad. It would be our last night together for a while, and we were uncertain about when we would meet again. We were deeply intimate and loving with each other. His every touch reassured me that we would be together for life. Our short but intense time together had bonded us for life. Distance doesn't matter when you love someone so deeply. We finally understood the meaning of soulmates. We realized what genuine love is: a single soul inhabiting two bodies.

The next morning, at 4 a.m., I was standing on the railway platform at Moradabad station. I wore his favourite red silk churidar suit as he wished to savour the image of me in that outfit during our separation. He had to catch a train to Jammu, from where he would proceed to Tangmarg and join the 1889 Light Regiment.

After Akhilesh left for his posting, I could sense Mummyji distancing herself from me. She was silent and ignoring me. She considered me the reason for her son's posting and as a result, putting his life at risk. My parents reached Moradabad in the morning, and Mummyji finally broke her silence. She told Ma, 'Your daughter will never wear her wedding lehenga ever again. Gift it to someone or discard it, but she will never wear it again!' At times, silence is the best answer. Superstitious beliefs sometimes takeover our logical thinking. I touched her feet while leaving, but I could still feel her resentment towards me.

I felt wretched about the way things had turned out, and was deeply hurt by the situation. I was weeping continuously. Then Ma held my hands, and said calmly, 'Don't worry, God will take care, and everything will be all right. Remain positive.'

I calmed myself, closed my eyes and worked on my inner strength. I knew that the role of an army wife was challenging. We believe the principles of army life but also have to follow the rituals of civil society. To maintain a balance between husband, in-laws, parents and the community, we have to face the situations life throws at us, with a smile. Soon, Akhilesh and I were on separate tracks of life. His jeep was reaching Tangmarg, and my car was heading towards Dehradun. Both carrying the hope to meet again.

FORWARD MARCH

In the darkest hour, when the demons come, call on me brother, and we will fight them together.

Nothing in this world can measure the emotions of a soldier. The task that takes them far from their loved ones soon becomes a reason for their excitement too. This sincere and dutiful trait often overpowers the gloomy heart of a soldier. His love for his nation doesn't keep him forlorn for too long.

Near a tiny village of Tangmarg, on both sides of a single road, and under the canopy of tall Chinar trees, the 1889 Light Regiment created their base for operations. The unit was operating from temporary structures, with the officers' tents on one side of the road, and tents for soldiers and other ranks on the other side. The regiment was responsible for counter-insurgency operations. The commanding officer, Lt Col Girish Kumar Mediratta, along with the other three officers of the regiment, received Capt. Akhilesh at the make-shift officers' mess.

A week later, at 4 a.m. when it was still dark outside, Akhilesh and 30 soldiers stealthily moved on foot towards a nearby village for a cordon and search operation. They'd received information about some intruders hiding there, planning a huge militancy operation. They sealed the three entrance roads of the village, leaving four soldiers at each gate. Then, Akhilesh and the rest of the soldiers reached the mosque in the centre of the village. At 6 a.m., an announcement from the mosque woke everyone up. The maulvi asked the villagers to come out of their houses and assemble in the field nearby. This was a common drill when the army visited a village, in search of terrorists. People were aware of this drill and gathered in the field within an hour. Everyone was carrying an identity card, which proved that they belonged to the village. Leaving behind six soldiers for the safety of the villagers, Akhilesh moved into the village with the rest of the soldiers, searching each house. Though the information received was about one or two intruders, they had to be prepared for more. They proceeded with great caution as the enemy could fire at the soldiers from any direction, house, window or door. The hidden terrorists knew the army was looking for them. They could have been hiding inside trunks or closets, to suddenly open fire on the soldiers. Soldiers risk their lives to nullify the damage that terrorists inflict on society. Around 8 a.m., Akhilesh sensed movement on the first floor of a house. He warned Naik Hari Singh and the others to take cover. The troops advanced towards the house.

Capt. Akhilesh climbed the wall from the side lane and reached the front door. It was locked from inside. Naik Hari Singh opened fire, targeting the window of the first floor. The terrorists fired back in reaction, confirming their presence in the house. After a few rounds of fire, the terrorists stopped firing. Now, it was a puzzling situation; had they run out of bullets and ammunition or saved some for later? By now, a few other soldiers joined Capt. Akhilesh at the front door. They broke down the door and entered the house. One terrorist jumped from the rear window of the first floor into the neighbour's house and made his way into the nearby forest by moving through the small clusters of houses. He seemed familiar with his escape route. While making his escape, he opened fire on the soldiers with his light machine gun (LMG). Their suspicions turned out to be true; the terrorists had saved some rounds to use at the end. The soldiers then combed through all the houses but found no other terrorists. Except for a few minor injuries on the right hand of one soldier and the left leg of another, everyone was fine. The village was safe, and the soldiers returned to the regiment.

A few days later, an informer visited the regiment. He came to drop fresh rations and while unloading he spoke to Capt. Akhilesh in a whisper.

'Sir, I've received information again that there are militants in the village. They have been scaring and forcing villagers to help and support them. Sometimes, they pay the villagers to transfer weapons and ammunition from one place to another. They are slowly spreading their wings.'

Based on the received information, Capt. Akhilesh was asked to plan an operation. Immediately after that, Akhilesh approached the Qubic battery for planning.

'*Sahab, sab nahi hai. Kisi kisi kaam me vyast hai.* (Sir, all the men are not present. They are all busy with their assigned tasks),' informed Naik Singh.

'Call those who are present. We have to go right now,' ordered Capt. Akhilesh.

Around 11.30 a.m., once again with Naik Singh and a handful of soldiers, Akhilesh approached the village. The same drill was performed and some soldiers sealed the entrances of the village. Capt. Akhilesh and the rest of the soldiers visited the maulvi, who was a trusted informer of the army. He made the announcement from the mosque's loudspeaker, asking everyone to come out to the open ground with their identity cards. Akhilesh and his team conducted a vigorous search for four hours, hunting for the militants. Puzzled and tired, they moved from door to door, searching every corner and cupboard of the houses. But found nothing.

At last, Maulvi Sahab invited them to sit at his house. There was a charpai with a couple of wooden stools in the front veranda. Capt. Akhilesh sat on the charpai while the maulvi made himself comfortable on one of the stools.

'*Sahab, kisi ne galat information di hai, us din ke baad koi nahi aaya yahaan.* (Someone has given you the wrong information. No one has come here after that day),' the maulvi said.

Akhilesh quietly pondered for a few minutes, and then said, '*Aap sahi farma rahe hai.* (You are right). We should return.' After a pause, he added, 'But before going, we should complete our search. Yours is the only house remaining.'

'*Mai fauj ki bahut izzat karta hu. Aap naye aye ho. Mai toh khud information deta hu.* (I have great respect for the army. You are new here but I've have been an army informer myself),' the maulvi argued.

'Maulvi Sahab, we respect you too, but I have orders to search every single house.' The maulvi's hesitation raised Capt. Akhilesh's suspicions.

It was a small house with a big open space at the back, followed by a huge field. The soldiers searched every corner of the house, but it was clean. As they were about to leave, Capt. Akhilesh noticed a vast heap of crops in the corner of the yard. It looked as though it hadn't been touched for months.

Without a word, he signalled Naik Singh to search that as well. And then turned to the maulvi to apologize, in an attempt to divert his mind from the activity.

'I am sorry we've disturbed you. I should have trusted you,' Akhilesh said to the maulvi. At that exact moment, he heard a gunshot.

There was a small mud room inside the heap. As the soldiers removed some portions of the heap, the militants hiding inside fired at the soldier Ghanshayam Das. It was a narrow escape for Ghanshayam as he bent down. Immediately, all the soldiers took their positions to attack and raised their LMGs towards the militants. With the maulvi at dead centre target of Capt. Akhilesh's AK-47, there was no scope for escape, so they surrendered. Capt. Akhilesh brought back two intruders for further investigations to the regiment along with the maulvi, who had been trusted by a few officers before this incident. It was an enormous shock to everyone. Now, they understood why militants kept escaping during the last few operations.

Within a week, artillery brigade commander, Brigadier Lakhwinder Singh, visited the regiment. He appreciated Capt. Akhilesh and the other soldiers for their bravery. In the evening, when all the officers were having dinner together, the commander asked Capt. Akhilesh about his family and found out that he had gotten married just two months back. He then asked him to call his wife to stay with him, at least for the summer. Regiments in the field have limited resources. They had only two guest rooms at the brigade headquarters, which were primarily reserved for the top ranks. Capt. Akhilesh was new to the unit and the junior-most, yet the privilege was extended to him. The situation was awkward. No one could say anything to the commander, but a minor discomfort crept in.

Akhilesh called me to say, 'I will send you a train ticket. The brigade commander has given me permission, so you can stay here for a month. The train is from Raiwala, it has a compartment reserved only for armed forces personnel.'

All I could say was, 'Love you!' to express my immense happiness. It was a pleasant surprise; I looked forward to joining Akhilesh at his new regiment in Tangmarg. The reservation was for the coming week. I planned to travel with Mrs Prasoon, as she too was joining her fauji husband for the summer.

Unaware of the conspiracy being hatched by Pakistan in the faraway mountains of Ladakh, towards the northern Line of Control (LOC) on the ridges of Kargil, Mushko Valley, Drass, Batalik and other sectors, the Indian troops marched towards their military outposts to check if the snow had retreated enough for the summer positions to be re-occupied. The military outposts on the ridges above the highway were 16,000–18,000 feet high. While winters are long and chilly, with temperatures often dropping to –50°C, these locations experience frigid nights in summer too. These posts are vacated in winter, and this practice has continued since 1971, when Pakistan faced defeat in the Indo–Pak war at the border of Rajasthan. The two nations signed the Simla Agreement in 1972, promising not to engage in armed conflict regarding the LOC between both countries.

On 14 May 1999, Captain Saurabh Kalia and five other soldiers – Sepoys Arjun Ram, Bhanwar Lal Bagaria, Bhika Ram, Moola Ram and Naresh Singh of the 4 Jat Regiment – were on a routine patrol of the Bajrang Post in the Kaksar sector, Kargil. They suddenly went missing after engaging in a fire-fight with Pakistani forces across the LOC. Later, Pakistan's Radio Skardu announced the capture of Indian soldiers by a platoon of Pakistani rangers. This news reached Indian media channels and spread like wildfire. Every citizen of India was worried and frightened by the news of missing soldiers. I too heard this news on television, which confirmed that something dangerous and suspicious was happening at the border.

Pakistani government authorities denied the news and claimed that they were Indian locals who had turned rebellious and were fighting for a free Kashmir. But the reality was different. During the winter of 1998–1999, the Pakistan Armed Forces secretly sent trained Pakistani troops and paramilitary forces into Indian Territory. They were disguised as mujahideen and arrived under white covers to blend into the snow and deceive intelligence observers. The infiltration was code-named 'Operation Badr'. It aimed to disconnect the link between Kashmir and Ladakh and compel Indian forces to withdraw from the Siachen Glacier, thus forcing India to negotiate a settlement of the broader Kashmir dispute.

The information reached the Chief of Army Staff, General V.P. Malik, with the suspicion that these might be rebellious jihadis. He ordered Headquarters Northern Command and its formation commanders to operate accordingly. Indian National Highway (NH1) connects Srinagar to Leh and passes through Kargil. From the ridgeline, the intruders could effectively dominate NH1 and seriously impede vehicular movement on the highway. Every summer, after the Zojila Pass opens, this highway is the lifeline extensively used for carrying civil and military traffic. The Indian Army carries the winter stock of essential commodities for the Ladakhis and military garrisons through this highway. Therefore, the early clearance of intruders from Tololing and its adjacent mountaintops was given the highest operation priority.

On 17 May 1999, the Indian Army inducted the 56th Mountain Brigade of the 8th Mountain Division into Drass, and handed them the responsibility of the eviction operation in the sector. Army infantry battalions moved first for the operation, as they are the most effective arm in mountain terrain. Northern Command assigned the preliminary operations task to 1 Naga Battalion. They launched a series of attacks on the Tololing and Point 5140 complex, and each time, the enemy nipped them down. The enemy had the advantage of being at a much greater height and sometimes, they didn't bother using ammunition and just rolled down boulders instead. The Nagas were the victims of such tactics. As the Indian soldiers with simple jungle boots and rifles slung on their shoulders were climbing up with the help of a rope, the enemy rolled down rocks, crushing them. The Nagas achieved some success in uncovering the enemy location, but at a high cost.

Estimating only six to eight intruders occupying some features on Tololing ridgeline, the 56th Mountain Brigade entrusted 18 Grenadiers to evict the intruders. They gave the battalion just four days to carry out reconnaissance, conduct acclimatization training for high-altitude conditions, and prepare for the attack. The regiments received orders to grip these intruders' by the neck and drag them out of the Indian forward posts.

On 22 May 1999, the 18 Grenadiers launched the attack with mortar fire and medium machine guns (MMGs) in support. When the troops got closer to the feature, a heavy volume of artillery shelling descended directly upon them. To their surprise, the enemy was using heavy machine guns (HMGs), MMGs and air defence (AD) guns. Many soldiers of the 18 Grenadiers were martyred, and the rest suffered splinter injuries. It was then that the brigade realized that they weren't pitted against jihadi militants but trained soldiers of the Pakistani Army, who were not in uniform. The Indian Army then figured that hundreds of Pakistani soldiers could have established fortified positions on the peaks of Kargil, deep inside the Indian portion of the LOC, with sophisticated equipment and supply lines into Pakistan.

The news reached the Defence Ministry within a few hours, and the Indian Army moved in more troops from Kashmir Valley to Kargil Sector. Now, all the brigades under Northern Command received information about the conflict between the two countries. However, on the international front, Pakistan continued to deny the presence of their soldiers on the LOC. This was when 'Operation Vijay' was announced within the Indian military, with instructions that no Indian soldier was to cross the LOC, as it had not yet been established whether or not the intruders sitting on our forward post were Pakistani guerrillas.

The news of the missing platoon of Capt. Kalia and martyred soldiers alarmed the officers and soldiers of the Indian Army. Regiments were ready to join the conflict, save their comrades and snatch back their country's forward post, and so was Capt. Akhilesh. The news filled this young officer with resentment and uneasy thoughts. The enemy had encroached into our national territory, captured all the heights and occupied dominating positions along NH1. They were threatening to cut Leh–Ladakh off from India and challenge the integrity of our nation. He remembered the oath from his passing out parade: *The safety, honour and welfare of our country come first, always and every time. The honour, welfare and comfort of the men I command come next. My ease, comfort, and safety come last, always and every time.* He decided he would join the action at the LOC at the first opportunity he could get. And his wish came true. The 1889 Light Regiment soon received orders to move to Kargil, and Capt. Akhilesh knew it would be difficult to break this news to his new bride. He kept thinking, *Will she understand? How will she react? She won't be prepared for this news. She is going to be frightened.*

The news of relentless gunfire along the LOC was now clear to the citizens of India thanks to television broadcasts. There was a big screen in one of the classrooms at my computer centre, which was used to teach students 3D and 2D animation. I had it moved to the centre lobby on the students' request and for myself as well. I didn't want to miss any news from the LOC.

The single long ring on the landline phone indicated an outstation call, so I knew it was from Akhilesh. He said, 'We are going away for training. I won't be able to call you for a few days. Don't worry. I will call you whenever it is possible.' He paused, and then continued, 'I have cancelled your train reservation ticket for 26 May. I hope you will understand.' He hid the truth about his regiment receiving orders to move to the LOC.

'I understand, it's your duty. Excel at whatever task is assigned to you. I will wait for you to return. You take care of yourself and don't worry about me.' I too hid the truth about knowing what the situation at Kargil was like and being aware of the regiment's movements. I didn't want him to feel stressed or worry about me.

Surprised at my response, Capt. Akhilesh remarked, 'Wow! You sound like a hardcore army wife. Who would guess you've been in the army for such a short duration? I'm happy you've adapted to the conditions so quickly. Thank you so much. This is such a relief.'

'A month-long exposure in the army has taught me how to support my husband. I love the way army women manage their homes and the welfare of the unit. I will live up to those standards and not disappoint you.'

'Thank you again for being so understanding. I love you and will return to you soon after completing my task.' I could hear the appreciation in his voice.

I said, 'I love you. I'll be fine as long as you're okay, so for the both of us, take care of yourself.'

My hands were shaking as I put down the receiver. I could hear my heart beating much louder, scared for Akhilesh. My anxiety was turning into reality, misfortune had already entered my life. Many negative thoughts popped into my mind and my eyes turned moist. Struggling to stay calm, I took a few deep breaths and closed my eyes for a while. But negative thoughts continued to flood my mind. When things are not under my control and I feel helpless, I rely on prayers. I believed in the power of thoughts, so I convinced myself to think positive – someone from the sky would protect my loved one when he was far away. I have faith in Lord Vishnu, so I began fasting on Thursdays for Akhilesh's safety.

I travelled with Papa from Dehradun to the Raiwala railway station to drop Mrs Prasoon on 26 May. Her husband was Akhilesh's senior in the same brigade. She confirmed my fears when she said, 'I'm sorry you won't be travelling with me to join Akhilesh. He has received orders to move to Kargil, where the shelling is on. Conditions are not good at the border. There are whispers that these are not militants but regular Pakistani soldiers.'

Papa and I returned home with heavy hearts. I smiled weakly in a feeble attempt to reassure Ma that everything was all right. I tried to shake off my gloomy mood. It was my duty to keep Akhilesh calm as he was the one who had to fight and perform his duty. Being deeply loved by someone gives you strength, while loving someone deeply requires courage. My worries for him were natural. I wanted to be with him, take care of him, and keep him motivated. I was not with him, and there wouldn't be any phone calls for a while either, so I started writing a letter to him every day.

Phoolon ke rang se, dil ki kalam se,
Tujhko likhi roz paati....

These lyrics perfectly expressed my emotions on being separated from my beloved. I also recorded a few romantic songs on an audio cassette and sent it to Akhilesh along with a Walkman and headphones. Each dispatch was addressed to: Captain Akhilesh Saxena, 1889 Light Regiment, C/O 56 APO.

PEAKS OF FIRE

Every warrior knows before he goes into battle,
how the little battle he is to fight fits into the larger picture,
And how the success of his fighting will influence
the war as a whole.

The convoy of 40 army trucks and 105-mm guns of the Indian Artillery passed through the Zojila Pass, heading towards Kargil. Capt. Akhilesh, Naik Shyamanand Divedi and driver R. Gwate led the 1889 Light regiment in one of the jeeps. After a 13-hour journey, the regiment deployed near Draupadi Kund – a small pond surrounded by snow-capped peaks and blue sky, with the milky way spread like a celestial glacier above the eastern horizon, its reflection faintly visible on the still, dark surface of the lake – at a distance of 18 km from Drass.

That evening, the commander of the artillery brigade of 8th Mountain Division, Brigadier Singh, had a brief meeting with the officers on updates in the Drass sector.

At Drass, a single road (NH-1) runs at the base of Tololing Mountain. On one side of the road is the Tololing peak, which is 16,000 feet high, a vast grassland without trees, and a few boulders scattered at the base. On the other side is the Sura River, 185-km long, which flows parallel to the road through the Kargil district. The enemy, sitting in the dominant position on the ridgeline – Tololing, Hump and Point 5140 – was the most severe threat. The road was at the direct target of heavy artillery shelling by the enemy. Any movement on the road was visible from the height. They had already damaged the Indian ammunition dump in Kargil. In the pitch darkness of the nights, Indian soldiers had recently constructed a wall of rocks to defend the vehicles and troops at the side of the road. The enemy had already damaged it in some places.

It was important to review the previous operations carried out at the location so as to plan further action. So, the officers at the meeting thoroughly investigated the steps they had already taken to retrieve their forward posts from the intruders; the results were alarming.

22 May: Assault by 18 Grenadiers. Because of the heavy volume of enemy artillery shelling, we lost many men. The bodies of our soldiers were still lying dead on the slopes of the mountain.

25 May: The Indian Government approved the use of Air Power about three weeks after the first reports of trouble. The Indian Air Force joined the ground troops of the Indian army in the Kargil War with Operation Safed Sagar or White Sea. Prior to this the government had only approved fighter and helicopter reconnaissance missions. The IAF Helicopters had also carried out casualty evacuation from Matayan on 21 May.

26 May: Assault by 18 grenadiers was carried out in consonance with IAF air strikes. The government, while clearing the use of air power, had banned the fighter jets from crossing the LOC under any circumstances. On 26th of May the IAF fielded MiG 21, 23 & 27 Squadrons, Jaguars and Armed Mi 17 helicopters from Srinagar, Awantipur and Adampur. This was the first time since the 1971 war that

fighter jets were being deployed. IAF too was not ready for the execution of such attacks from altitudes as high as 30,000 feet to engage ground targets at an altitude of 15 ~ 17,000 feet. It was unprecedented – nowhere in the world had such an aerial engagement taken place earlier. Apart from the challenges of manoeuvring the aircraft in thin air to see and attack the enemy positions, the weapon ballistics were totally different as compared to what had been practiced in air to ground ranges in the plains.

27 May: Squadron Leader K. Nachiketa's formation of 4 x MiG 27 aircraft from 9 Squadron was detailed to strike targets in the Batalik sector with 80 MM Rockets. The targets were at altitudes over 17,000 feet. After firing his Rockets in the first pass he came for another pass, this time firing from his 30 MM cannon. During this pass his aircraft flamed out and he had to eject over enemy-held territory; upon landing he was captured and became a prisoner of war (POW). His formation leader orbited over his crash site for some time trying to locate him, for a search and rescue (SAR) helicopter to come and pick him up. Now that his aircraft was low on fuel, he radioed for help to Srinagar. Squadron Leader Ahuja and his number 2 Flying Officer P.G. Reddy flying MiG 21 aircraft of 17 Squadron were waiting for take-off at Srinagar airfield. Upon hearing this call for help, they volunteered to take his place as they were supposed to carry out photo reconnaissance of the same target for bomb damage assessment (BDA). Upon reaching the target area, the MiG 27 pilot warned Ahuja that the enemy had been firing surface to air missiles (SAMs). He acknowledged the information about this danger and set up orbit over the normal engagement envelope of Man Portable Surface to Air Missiles. He made

R/T (Radio Telephony) contact with a Cheetah Pilot flying over Kargil and gave him the location of the crash site, guiding him to come and pick up Nachiketa. After some time, his Number 2, Flying Officer P.G. Reddy reported that his aircraft was running low on fuel. Ahuja asked him to go back to base. However, in his exuberance to keep the crash site in contact to facilitate a successful SAR of Flight Lieutenant Nachiketa, his aircraft descended and lost altitude and was shot down by an enemy Stinger Surface to Air Missile. He too ejected in enemy-held territory where he was captured and killed in captivity.

28 May: At 11.30 a.m., a formation of 4 helicopters attacked the Tololing peak in the Drass sector. An enemy stinger missile shot them down, killing all four crew members. These losses forced the IAF to reassess its strategy, and they immediately withdrew the armed helicopters from offensive roles.

28 May: 18 Grenadiers created a base 300 metres below Tololing peak. The enemy fire could not reach them, as they were on the same slope behind enormous boulders. Weak but not shattered, they planned another furious assault on the dense foggy night of 28 May. Under the leadership of Maj. Rajesh Singh Adhikari, B Company reached within 25–30 metres of the enemy's sangar (a temporary structure constructed of stones, sandbags, or gabions for the fortified position with a breastwork). Suddenly, mist disappeared and they found themselves surrounded by the enemy. An intense close-combat battle erupted, during which the enemy killed Maj. Adhikari, Subedar Randhir Singh, Lance Naik R.K. Yadav and Grenadier Parveen Kumar. They pushed the rest back. The enemy was reinforcing Tololing Top from Point 5140, which was just behind and

at a greater height. Captain Sachin Nimbalkar, Lieutenant Balwant Singh and their troops followed Maj. Adhikari to lend support but got stuck behind a boulder on the tiny ledge of a sheer cliff face, for three days.

30 May: The IAF inducted the Mirage 2000 fleet. It was the best aircraft in the IAF inventory, capable of optimum performance under high-altitude conditions. It was initially armed with 250-kg 'dumb' bombs meant to take out a target, but it still posed some risks. A near miss target by a mile could result in casualties among their own troops. These were then modified to deliver laser-guided bombs and by 12 June were ready to attack targets located on mountain tops with precision. The attacks on Tiger Hill and the Muntho Dhalo supply camp were some of the notable successes of the Mirage 2000 fleet.

2 June: Regimental pride was at stake. The martyrdom of his junior officer filled Lieutenant Colonel Ramakrishnan Vishwanathan with anger. He was second-in-command of the 18 Grenadiers, and launched another assault. The men reached the top after a rigorous six-hour climb. They were trying to retrieve the body of Maj. Adhikari but were unable to reach that far. There was enemy fire everywhere. They lost nine men in the fire-fight. A little while later, Lt Col Vishwanathan was also hit. The commanding officer, Col Khushal Thakur moved up when he received information from the radio operator, and somehow dragged Lt Col Vishwanath to safety, but it was too late. Lt Col Vishwanathan breathed his last in the laps of his CO. It was a suicidal attack, he knew he would die.

There was dismay and gloom all around. Twenty-five soldiers, including officers from the unit, were martyred. The death of his young officers and soldiers shattered

Col Thakur. The bodies of Maj. Adhikari and his wireless operator were still lying on the battlefield. In grief and pain, Col Thakur decided not to leave without the bodies of his men. With limited food resources, ammunition and men, he stayed on the base.

The situation was miserable. With all attempts having failed, our soldiers were sinking into a despondent state. They were wounded and broken over losing their buddies, but not yet discouraged. They silently evacuated the injured soldiers under the blanket of the dark night. It was a risky, back-breaking and painful process, but the army never leaves their buddies behind. Our soldiers would hide under scattered boulders and rugged rocks for cover during the daytime. Every night, they toiled tirelessly to ferry food and ammunition up to a certain height and bring back the wounded. They were thirsty, hungry and dejected, but still crawled and climbed inch by inch along the steep incline with the wind howling around them, and temperatures ranging between –5 and –11 degrees centigrade.

By now, the Indian Army had realized the gravity of the situation. Enemy artillery fire was accurate and continuous, which confirmed that these were not militants but Pakistan military, but we had no proof. We had suffered enough just by denying the facts conveyed by our troops at the front. We had failed in intelligence and planning. It was no longer just a conflict between militants and Indian Infantry units. It was actually an undeclared war between India and Pakistan, who had masked their soldiers as militants without uniforms. Finally, the 8th Mountain Division under Major General Mohinder Puri took over command of Drass on 1 June 1999. On 2 June, the artillery brigade was called under the command of Brigadier Singh to make their grip for the

Kargil War. And as a part of the artillery brigade, the 1889 Light Regiment was deployed near Draupadi Kund. Next, a meeting of all the artillery officers was called to understand the severity of the current situation and to prepare the plan of action for victory.

'We will live up to our motto, the motto of the regiments of the Indian Artillery – *Sarvatra Izzat o Iqbal.* Yes, everywhere with honour and glory. We will prove it in the face of war,' all the officers pledged loudly.

After the brigade meeting, the officiating CO of the 1889 Light Regiment called all the regiment officers to his tent and addressed them:

'Now, you are well aware of the situation, conditions are pretty serious in Drass. Our infantry units failed in our many attempts to capture Tololing peak. Recently, 2 Rajputana Rifles has been assigned to carry out further assaults to capture the Tololing ridge. They have asked for Indian Artillery support. The artillery brigade gave us the responsibility to provide the artillery fire and FOO. Who would like to join 2 Rajputana Rifles in the Drass sector?'

Without delay, Capt. Akhilesh volunteered to join his infantry brothers in Drass.

'Tomorrow early morning, with your FOO team, report to the commanding officer of 2 Rajputana Rifles, Colonel M.B. Ravindranath. His regiment is acclimatizing at Matayen.'

'Right, sir.' Capt. Akhilesh accepted the orders without delay.

From the moment Capt. Akhilesh received an update about the Drass sector, he wanted to join his comrades there. He moved towards his tent to organize his backpack. He took a combat uniform and a few essential items for daily use. He always carried two photo frames with him: one with a picture of his wife and the other of his parents. They were his entire world, and now it was time to leave them behind and move forward to fight the enemy for the pride of his country. He kept looking at the photo frames as though he wanted to convey his feelings to them. Somewhere underneath the Indian Army uniform, the preparation since childhood for a purpose and the pledge at the time of his passing out, his heart did beat for his wife and parents too. He was a loving husband and a sincere son who wanted to live with his wife and care for his parents. As he was putting the photo frames into his bag, he found a long, thick strand of black hair on his uniform in the trunk. He remembered when Shikha was packing his trunk, he had hugged her reassuringly and said, 'I will be okay. Your love is a protective shield for me.' She had placed her head on his chest without a word, struggling to hold back her tears. It was her hair. Waves of emotion overwhelmed Akhilesh and his eyes were moist, but his priority was still crystal clear. He had to fight for his country, and nothing could deviate him from his target. With a gloomy heart, he took a deep breath, pushed back the emotions, and shifted his focus to loading his weapons for the journey.

On 3 June, at 7 a.m., a jeep left Draupadi Kund and headed towards Matayen, 27 km from the main Drass village. The regiment of 2 Rajputana Rifles was acclimatizing here for the attack, which was planned for 12 June. Even on the insistence of higher authorities, the CO of the regiment took a stand not to go directly to the battlefield and requested a few days for the preparation of the attack. Learning a lesson from the failed attacks on Tololing, Col. Ravindranath stood up for his men and insisted on Indian Artillery support for the attack. According to him, 'I can't just throw my men into the war zone without even basic preparation. Well-planned is half done.'

Leaving driver R. Gwate and Naik Shyamanand Divedi in the jeep, Capt. Akhilesh reported to the commanding officer of 2 Rajputana Rifles.

'Welcome, Akhilesh. We've been waiting for you,' the colonel said while shaking hands with Capt. Akhilesh.

'After several attempts, 18 Grenadiers failed to capture Tololing peak, and now the brigade has called 2 Rajputana Rifles for the same task. When I was going into the meeting with the commander, Colonel Alok Deb from an artillery regiment was coming out from the same room. He had a briefing with the commander just before my meeting. The tension and worry were obvious from his face. He saw me and advised, "Don't accept a task you can't execute". At the time, I could not relate to the severity of the task, but after receiving a brief, I am genuinely worried,' said Col Ravindranath. 'As an infantry officer, I know our vision is within limits. But artillery gunners will always have deep insight into the condition. They can see beyond. One should always listen to the advice of an artillery officer carefully.'

Capt. Akhilesh was listening to the senior officer attentively.

'Sir, I am honoured to be a gunner and have chosen to support my infantry comrades.'

'Yes, Akhilesh. It's a serious responsibility. Infantry alone can't achieve it. We require the support of gunners. I require your full dedication as you are the ones who can damage enemy bunkers before we reach there and also protect us while we climb up the peak,' Col. Ravindranath said with hope.

'Sir, I will not disappoint you. We will create an undefeatable fire plan. This time the enemy will repent,' Capt. Akhilesh sounded like an angry lion.

'While you plan, keep in mind that those who have captured our posts are not militants but trained soldiers of the Pakistani Army, supported by artillery guns. This is not an insurgency operation but a full-fledged war. We have suffered enough because of confusion, but we know the reality on the ground, unfortunately, we don't have evidence yet to show it to the authorities,' briefed the colonel.

'Okay, sir. We will plan for a war attack. Sir, I have to see Tololing to create an artillery fire plan,' Capt. Akhilesh requested.

Col Ravindranath ordered Havaldar Sarman Singh of 2 Rajputana Rifles to accompany him.

The artillery officer must be aware of the enemy's location. He has to gather a good deal of information before creating a fire plan. Capt. Akhilesh's jeep headed towards Drass town. It was a narrow and lonely road with majestic scenic beauty. On one side there were hillocks on a carpet of grass, and on the other side, the river flowed parallel to the road. From a specific location, Capt. Akhilesh saw an extensive wall on the side of the road towards the side of the mountains. Many army vehicles were parked on the highway, with one side touching the wall. They were using the wall as a cover shield.

'Sarman, the entire 8th Mountain Division is in Drass, but why can't I see anyone?' asked Capt. Akhilesh.

'Sir, the soldiers must sit quietly inside the trucks or behind the boulders the entire day, else the enemy may shoot at us,' Havaldar Singh explained.

'What? Can they see us?' Capt. Akhilesh was shocked.

'Yes, sir,' replied Havaldar Singh, and within a minute, an artillery shell dropped just a few metres ahead of the jeep.

'Park the jeep at the side of the wall. They are observing our movements,' Havaldar Singh shouted to the driver.

'Oh my God! The enemy is sitting right on the top of this hill. I think it is at least 15 km inside LOC.' Puzzled and angry, Capt. Akhilesh looked towards the mountain.

'Yes, sir. This is Tololing peak.'

'I had the information but never imagined it was so close. We are sitting at target for the enemy guns,' remarked Capt. Akhilesh.

'Yes, sir. Any day could be our last day, but we will not die without fighting,' said Havaldar Singh.

'Not even while fighting. Let the enemy die for their country,' Capt. Akhilesh said emphatically.

It was like sitting on the mouth of a volcano. The locals had left their homes and moved far away from the LOC due to the heavy firing. There were only empty houses remaining in the village. The Indian Army provided shelter and food to the people who had stayed behind to help and support. Soldiers were surviving with the bare minimum; sleeping, eating and living between the ridges of boulders or in trucks; anywhere they could hide during the day. Bathing and shaving were possible only once in a few weeks, whenever they came down to base.

The conditions were severe and we needed to win as soon as possible, with just six weeks in hand. After August, winter would set in, and temperatures would plummet to –30 degrees centigrade. All the approaching routes to the army posts would get covered in snow. Later, in the freezing surroundings, it would be an impossible task. Once winter began, we would not be able to approach Leh–Ladakh. As a result, the enemy would torture and kill our buddies in Leh and erase Leh–Ladakh from the map of our country. This time, we wanted to make a plan for sure-shot success. Every step towards victory had to be taken cautiously.

Building up success for the Tololing attack at Drass sector:

Modification in Indian Air Strikes

Wing Commander Birender Singh Dhanoa (now Retired Air Chief Marshal) was the Commander of 17 Squadron 'Golden Arrows'. His squadron was the only dedicated Fighter Reconnaissance (FR) Squadron of the Indian Air Force which was moved from Bathinda in the plains of Punjab to Srinagar on 18 May 1999. Initially, it was intended to carry out low level photo reconnaissance to help locate enemy positions inside the LOC, the first one was conducted on 21 May. This was like a life's mission for him and his squadron; one they had waited and tirelessly trained for. Being deployed for war was a dream he carried in eyes ever since he joined the NDA at the age of 17. Initial reconnaissance did reveal the locations of some enemy sangars, small in size and covered in snow which were very difficult to see and attack on from the air. After initial losses to Surface to Air Missiles – one fighter and a helicopter – the IAF changed the role of the squadron from Low Level FR to High Altitude GPS assisted bombing, which he planned carefully with his team. They realized that during such bombing missions, a miss by a few metres could cause casualties among own troops poised for attacking enemy positions. So, when he was asked by his AOC-in-C Air Marshal Vinod Patney if he could attack those targets at night, he jumped at the opportunity and began devising innovative methods to attack the same targets at low level in the mountains. As the enemy had mainly deployed shoulder fired SAMs, they were ineffective at night in the mountains as radar cueing was not available to them. The MiG 21 aircraft would be flown when the snow-clad mountains were shining in the moonlight. This resulted in more accurate bombings and was a nuisance for the Pakistani troops as they were being bombed day and night under the cover of the clouds.

Preparation of Artillery Fire Plan

Gunners turned to the annals of history to study how famous warriors such as Babar and Ranjit Singh used rows of master gunners to fire cannonballs directly at the enemy. If they could use the simplest tubes in controlled direct firing, why couldn't sophisticated gun systems be utilized the same way? This was one of the most innovative artillery tactics to win a war. For the first time in Indian military history, guns such as Bofors were used in a direct firing role to first soften up the enemy and then provide the infantry the opportunity for the final assault. The strategy was to fire at the enemy's position regularly until our troops found their way up the hill. The guns that they directed for fire were 40 km away, and scattered. There was a team of 10 gunmen (artillery soldiers) at the gun location. Their job was to fire towards the coordinates directed by FOO, and immediately move the guns to a different location to handle the enemy's counter fire. The artillery officers planned to use 20 artillery fire units simultaneously on the target. Each unit contained either six Bofors guns or six 105-mm artillery guns. So, in the initial phase, there were only a few batteries of 105-mm guns, but by the end of the first week of June, 155-mm Bofors guns started moving in. As the enemy had a good line of sight of the highway from the peaks, our troops deployed the massive guns after sunset. At thc Gunıri and Matayen bases, they moved the guns from the plains. In the dead of night, powerful Scania trucks pulled huge artillery guns to predetermined gun positions. The trucks moved with their lights switched off. Two soldiers trotted in front of the trucks, flashing torchlights to provide visualization of the outlines of the road and thc curves so the vehicles wouldn't drive into the deep gorge. They carved the gun locations out of the mountainside to provide accurate fire and avoid counter artillery fire from the enemy. By 7 June, the guns were deployed. As the time to launch the attack approached, soldiers worked in the biting cold at night to make sure all guns were ready for action. Anti-aircraft guns scanned the skies. Meanwhile, para commandos moved forward. Their job was to direct counter-battery fire if the troops encountered any Pakistani artillery firing.

Artillery officers of 197 field regiment and 1889 light regiment created a Fire Plan (FP) to control firing from 120 artillery guns on Tololing peak and named it 'Nischay Vijay'. It was now time for Forward observation officers

(FOO) to start climbing to vantage positions to direct the fire. Capt. Akhilesh was tasked to the role of FOO and to go with the infantry battalion uphill to execute the artillery Fire Plan. The operation was tough and required extreme precision. There was no room for error; a single mistake could ruin the entire mission.

On the morning of 8 June, Capt. Akhilesh, with his FOO team, Naik Shyamanand, Naik Dashrath and driver R. Gwate, left the unit location to join 2 Rajputana Rifles who were busy dumping ammunition at the firm base of Tololing Mountain.

Preparation of Infantry Regiment

The CO of 2 Rajputana Rifles asked for six days to plan and dump ammunition at the firm base. Observing the critical conditions, General Officer Commanding (GOC) approved the proposal. Initially, the regiment was around 400 soldiers strong, but climbing at 16,000 feet with weight was a strenuous task. Only young soldiers could move uphill due to the low oxygen levels, and most of the soldiers were struggling to breathe. Moreover, the soldiers were not familiar with the area; many tripped down the slippery slopes at night and got injured. So only 50% of soldiers were effectively working. They spent the entire night transporting ammunition, food and weapons uphill from Drass town to the firm base from where the regiment would launch the attack. By the third day, only 33% of the ammunition had reached uphill, which was a matter of concern for the CO.

Udham Singh was a carpenter in the unit. He observed the apprehension of his commanding officer and was desperate to support the task assigned to his regiment. He approached the quartermaster and said, 'Sahabji, let me help. I too will carry ammunition to the base.' The quartermaster ignored him. He approached his senior once again and was ignored the second time as well. While soldiers were struggling to climb on the cleft of the mountain at night, Singh repeatedly requested the quartermaster to let him to do it too.

When he asked for the fourth time, the quartermaster yelled, '*Abe aankh ke andhe, hum tujhe sambhalenge ya ammunition dump karenge?* (You blind fellow, do we look after you or dump the ammunition?)'

Udham Singh could see nothing at night, as he suffered from night blindness.

He replied gently, '*Sahab, darte kyun ho, mai aagewale ka coat pakad ke climb karunga and coat pakad ke hi vapas aunga.* (Sir, why are you afraid? I will hold the coat of a person in front of me while climbing uphill and come down the samc way).' And he did exactly that. Singh's dedication infused fresh energy into the others. After he joined the team, there wasn't a single jawan who made an excuse while dumping the ammunition to the base. And in just three days, all the ammunition and food supplies reached the desired location, and the battalion was ready to attack.

On 10 June, the newspaper headlines outraged every citizen of the country. I could not stop my tears at the institute lobby, when I read the newspaper, and felt shivers run through my entire body. I took the newspaper and rushed into my office but in my anxiety, I could not sit on the chair. I sat down on the carpeted floor and continued reading. The bodies of Capt. Kalia and five other team members of the 4 Jat Regiment, who had been missing since 14 May, were handed over to India on 9 June. The injuries to their body revealed that the soldiers had been tortured with burning cigarettes. The bodies were missing parts; their eyeballs were gouged out and their noses, ears and genitals were chopped off before the enemy shot them on their temples. Nobody had ever witnessed this kind of cruelty in the history of armed conflicts between the two countries. India expressed its outrage over the mutilation and disfigurement of six of its army personnel and termed it a 'violation of international conventions'.

I cried as I imagined the pain our soldiers would have gone through before dying. I felt helpless and prayed to God to take care of Akhilesh. My heart sank as he was on the same battlefield, and the brute face of the enemy was no longer hidden. Negative thoughts were dragging me down. I felt as though I was trapped inside a tiny room with black walls, and no door or window; just complete darkness wherein I couldn't even see my own hands. Akhilesh was in pain, calling my name for help from a distance. I tried to run to hold him, but I could not reach him. *What if he did not return from the battlefield? I would end my life. I had lost all interest in living in a world without him.* The sound of the phone ringing broke my macabre train of thoughts and brought me back to my senses. I picked up the receiver.

I heard my father on the other side. 'Your mother was feeling breathless, and became unconscious. I have brought her to the hospital. They have admitted her saying it was a stroke. I think she is worried about you.'

'I am coming, Papa. Don't worry. She will be all right.' I said in a flash.

This was like a wake-up call for me. I realized the two people I love the most now require my support and care: Akhilesh on the battlefield and Ma at the hospital. I had to pull myself together to take care of them. Courage was the only way out for me. I had to become a positive shield for Akhilesh so that no sad thoughts could reach him through me, and I didn't want Ma to see me crying either. I had to be there for Akhilesh's parents too. There was so much to handle. That night, I lit an oil lamp at my temple at home and promised to keep it burning until Akhilesh returned. I also vowed to fast every Thursday for the rest of my life, and prayed to God to keep him alive. I was the wife of a soldier who was ready to sacrifice his life for the country. Since that day, a silent prayer to end the war remained in my heart.

It was the first time the media played a significant role in unveiling the truth about Kargil. Everyone now knew that our soldiers were fighting an undeclared war. The brutality with which Capt. Kalia and his team were killed aroused the patriotic emotions of the citizens of our country, and grief soon turned into anger. I still remember people approaching the army headquarters in droves, requesting admission into the army to fight the enemy. They were willing to contribute in any way possible; as labourers, cooks, nurses. They were willing to fill any gap that existed. Now, I was not among the few writing letters to a soldier at the war front: innumerable people were writing to our jawans. I observed a strong reflection of patriotism in every citizen. Now, they no longer belonged to any religion or caste. Now, they were just Indians.

BATTLE OF TOLOLING

The harder the fighting and the longer the war, the more the infantry and all the arms lean on the gunners.

It was a terrible moment even for the bravest soldier who received the bodies of Capt. Kalia and five others from the Pakistani Army at Post 43 in the Kargil sector on 9 June. Indian soldiers sitting on the Kargil border were unclear who the intruders were, but they were clear about their conduct. Soon, the stories of enemy brutality became the main topic of discussion among the soldiers. 'They shoot straight in the face. If you're captured alive, they will torture you by stubbing lit cigarettes on your skin, puncture your eyes, fracture your bones and cut you into pieces before shooting you.' The morale of some junior soldiers had collapsed on hearing these gruesome details, while others were filled with anger and wanted to take revenge on the enemy. In both cases, the soldier could make mistakes, so they required visionary leadership. Other than gossip, some harsh truths were evident to the soldiers – the enemy sitting at the top could observe the activities at ground level. They had the advantage of height and had planted landmines on all the routes from the Indian side. This made attacks from the Indian side extremely difficult, and the actual chances of success were not even 2%. It was like a suicide mission and a litmus test for the youngest officers leading the troops.

Under normal circumstances in the army, officers command the troops from the middle for better coordination, but this time, the junior officers of the Indian Army decided to lead from the front. It was the only way to motivate and guide soldiers in such hostile conditions.

On the afternoon of 9 June, Col Ravindranath conducted a darbar (meeting) with all the regiment officers and soldiers to discuss the primary plan for the crucial assault. In the centre, there was a sand model of the entire Tololing ridge. The administrative officer briefed the regiment about the firebase, motor, ammunition and code of conduct. He gave straight instructions to everyone, 'Keep your last letter in your right pocket and the last bullet in your left pocket. You should never be captured by the enemy. If you think you are likely to get captured and have run out of ammunition, load this last bullet in your gun and kill yourself. It's our duty to remove the letter from the right pocket of a dead soldier's body and post it.' Finally, Col Ravindranath said, 'It will be a terribly sad moment for me, but I will shoot anyone who refuses to go for the assault. Mark my words; I will do that. There is no turning back. Not even for me. I have given you whatever you require, and now I want Tololing in return.'

Major Vivek Gupta got emotional and said, 'We will lead from the front, and officers will be the first to take the bullet of the enemy on their chest. We will show the enemy what courage is.'

Company Havaldar Major Yashvir Singh also got sentimental, 'Sir, I assure you on behalf of all the soldiers of 2 Rajputana Rifles. We will retain the glory of our regiment, even at the cost of our lives. No one will turn back. In true Rajput tradition, we all will wrap the kesariya bana (orange turban) around our heads with a promise to either emerge victorious or not come back at all, but we will not return in defeat. Jai Hind!'

It was noon on 10 June 1999. Capt. Akhilesh was in a sombre mood, sitting in the shade of a boulder, far from his home and loved ones. His eyes turned moist while writing the letter. It was his last letter to his parents and his newlywed bride. He was preparing for a suicide mission. All the memories flashed through his mind: his life, his dreams, the promises he made to his wife on his wedding day. His emotions overflowed, and his heart was filled with pain on realizing that he may die and never return to his family ever again. He fought back the fear that surged through him each time he thought about dying. But the fear started his mind churning again – he may not be able to support his parents in their old age or share life's joys and struggles with his wife. Soldiers knew they were closer to death with every step towards the peak, which meant potentially turning their wives into widows and having their families mourn the loss of a member. However, the entire nation was looking at them to redeem the prestige of the country. So, they had to gather courage, fight and achieve victory, even at the cost of their lives. He completed writing the letters, sealed them and placed them safely in his trunk, as he knew it would be sent to his home if he didn't make it. It is an unspoken tradition in the Indian Army that before every critical assault in a war, soldiers write a last letter to their loved ones. Higher authorities send this letter and the soldier's belongings to his family in the event that he does not return from the battlefield. If, by luck, he returns, he tears up the letter.

After writing his letters, Capt. Akhilesh wished to speak to his beloved.

A long ring on the phone made me aware that it was Akhilesh's call. I was waiting, since the last time I had spoken to him was 19 days ago.

'I just wanted to hear your voice. I hope you're well and everything is all right.' He sounded low.

'Yes, everything is fine. You take care of yourself. I call Moradabad regularly. Your parents are fine too. Neeraj is on vacation, so he often answers the phone.' I told him.

'Have you received my songs and Walkman?' I asked.

'Yes, I listen to it when I miss you, and I miss you all the time. The songs are apt for our situation.'

'Yes, I feel the same way.' I replied.

'I cannot call you again for a few weeks.' His voice now had me worried, but I had to keep my calm as I had decided earlier.

'I have full confidence in my God that you will be successful, and we will be together again,' I spoke with faith.

'I can't say when we will be together again.' The uncertainty of life was evident from his words. 'I love you and will keep loving you until my last breath,' he whispered.

'Same here. I love you and will keep loving you until my last breath,' I replied with tears in my eyes.

'The duty of a soldier is not to die for his country. You should be smart enough to make the enemy die for his. I will wait for you, and you will come back. *Tum bas josh me hosh nahi khona* (You just keep your head on your shoulders and don't get swayed by emotions),' I said without taking a breath.

While hanging up, Capt. Akhilesh thought, *Does she know I am going for an attack?* He hadn't told her anything about it, so why was she speaking this way? But her words infused him with renewed confidence and energy. He felt motivated and inspired to execute his duty. There was an inexplicable telepathy between us.

On 11 June 1999, Capt. Akhilesh, with his FOO team, registered all enemy positions again during the daytime so he could execute accurate and massive artillery fire on them. For many days and nights, he observed Tololing peak; how it looked during the day and how to recognize it in the darkest night. He was responsible for executing the artillery Fire Plan, 'Nischay Vijay', to its success. Artillery fire has a range of 30–40 km, and the job of the FO officer is to direct the fire to the correct location. Even a tiny error could be disastrous and end up killing our own troops. With the help of a compass, he marked Tololing peak on the grid lines of the map in hand, but in reality, the feature was massive. He ranged and directed two to three shots on the target, pinpointed an exact location on the map, and noted the accurate coordinates. But since the attack had to be started at night, the speed of wind, pressure and humidity could change the coordinates. Capt. Akhilesh silently prayed to the Almighty for the success of the mission. The responsibility was huge, and everyone was looking towards artillery fire with the hope to survive and win.

On the afternoon of 12 June, the battalions of 2 Rajputana Rifles were ready at the firm base for the Tololing attack. Major Amrinder Singh Kasana, an artillery battery

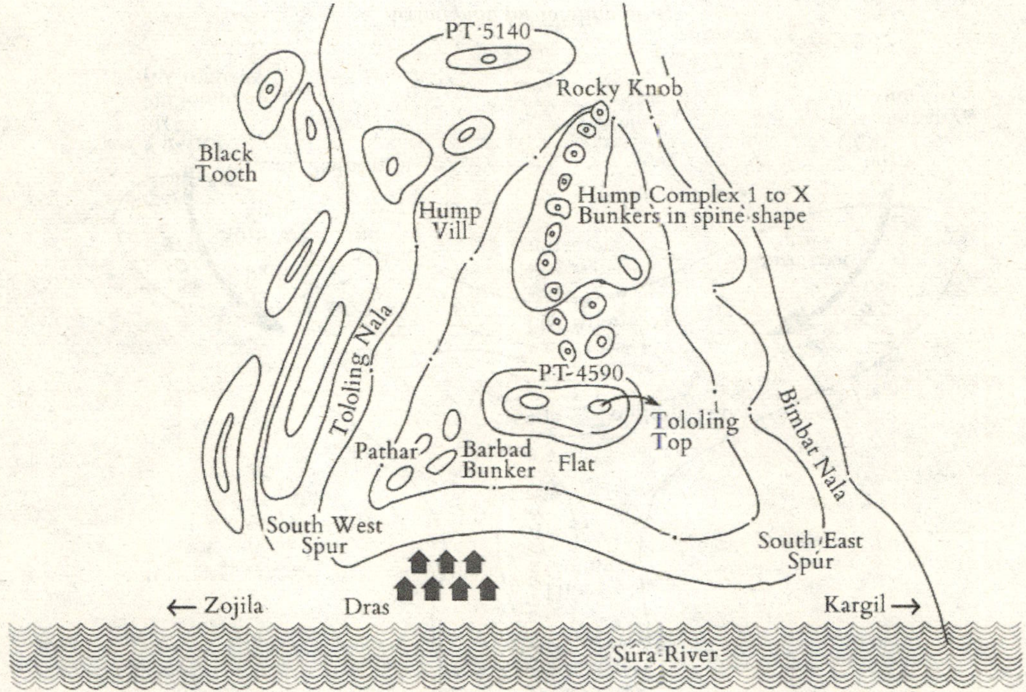

Structure of Tololing region (arial view)

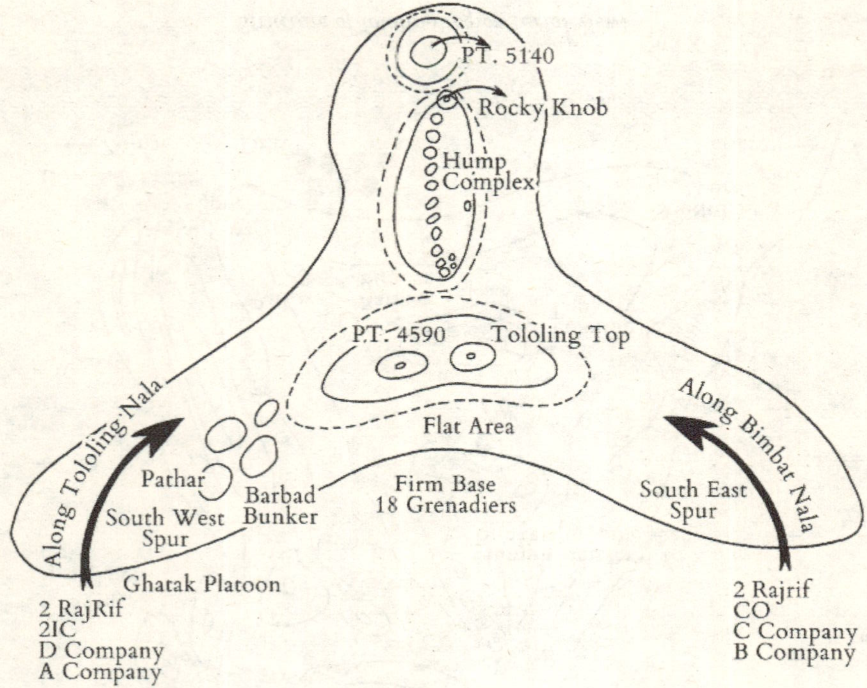

Action plan for Tololing attack

commander with 18 Grenadiers, volunteered to continue with 2 Rajputana Rifles. Col Ravindranath and Major Sandeep Bajaj, second in command, (2IC) of 2 Rajputana Rifles briefed the soldiers about the final action plan. They divided the Tololing complex into four major assault areas – Tololing Top, Point 4590, Flat Area and Barbad Bunker. There were two approaches towards Tololing peak; one from the southwest, along with Tololing nala, and another from the southeast, Bimbat nala. The leading companies would take separate paths for the attack. At the base of each path, there would be a waiting area for reserved companies. Maj. Bajaj would direct the assault from the southwest ridge, and the CO would take control on the southeast ridge. Delta Company, led by Major Mohit Saxena, would go first, towards Point 4590 from the southwest ridge, to cut off the enemy's retreat. Capt. Akhilesh would start moving up with Delta Company as he had to execute and control the entire artillery fire plan, keeping two leading companies at his sides to provide cover to both the companies. Charlie Company, led by Maj. Gupta, would go straight up to Tololing Top through Bimbat nala from the southeast ridge. Artillery officer Captain M.K. Singh would accompany Charlie Company. Bravo Company would start moving towards the flat ridge after 50 minutes of Charlie Company, and Alpha Company, led by Maj. Acharya, would stay reserved on base until they received the signal to climb. Captain N. Kengurüse, with his commando platoon, would block Pakistani firing from the Hump as this feature was 500 metres higher on the same ridge. The Grenadiers would provide covering fire against Pakistan on the nearby ridges.

Before the assault and after the puja of Karni Mata, which soldiers perform before any dangerous mission, Col Ravindranath assembled his regiment to boost their morale. He stood up and said, 'The Rajputana Rifles is one of the oldest rifle regiments. Now is the time to establish your name in golden letters in the history of our regiment. Your actions will decide how the citizens of our country remember you. Rajputs never accept defeat; they win or die. Now, the legacy of our regiment is on your shoulders. I will wait for your message and come to Tololing peak when you have established the tricolour on it. Jai Hind!'

Maj. Gupta encouraged his troops. 'If victory is certain, even a coward can win, but the real brave one dares to fight even when he knows his victory is near impossible. Victory is reserved for those who are ready to pay its price. Jai Hind!'

Along with Lieutenant Praveen Singh Tomar, there were 11 Tomars. Havaldar Yashvir Singh Tomar said, '*Sahib gyarah ja rahe hain aur gyarah jeet kar lautenge* (Sir, 11 Tomars are going and 11 will return victorious)'.

Maj. Saxena said, 'Get ready to continue the legacy of your unit. The entire country is looking at you to restore our honour.'

Junior Commissioned Officer (JCO) Bhanwar Lal assured his commanding officer, 'Sir, have breakfast with us tomorrow morning. We will wait for you on Tololing Top.'

Capt. Akhilesh said, 'Let us make a promise to ourselves not to die in an accident or succumb to any disease. Rather, we will go down in glory. Future generations will remember us with pride. I will direct a heavy shower of shelling on the enemy and make sure the head of the enemy remains down until you all reach the peak. After that, I will fight as an infantry officer and remain as a shield in front of all of you. Jai Hind!'

Josh (energy) was in the air. Indian troops wanted to shout 'Jai Hind', but because of the proximity of the enemy, they just saluted their officers. The gravity and importance of their attack were apparent to the soldiers. This time, Indian troops were not ready to accept defeat. Now, action would speak louder than words.

All the troops dispersed to collect their weapons and ammunition to get ready for the final assault, while Subedar Major raised his hand requesting the CO, 'Sir, I wanted to mention three important points to all the officers leading the attacks. May I?'

The CO replied graciously, 'Yes, Sahab, please go ahead.'

The Subedar Major was the oldest and most experienced soldier there. All the officers stayed back to listen to him attentively. 'Sirs, I am speaking from my own experience, and wish you all to stay alive and live long lives. You must keep these three important points in mind:

1. The leader, officer-in-charge, or commander should himself check the reality on the ground before reporting to his senior if any information has come to him. Don't just believe what you are told and execute before checking the truth. I have experienced this in the history of our regiment, and we have suffered significant losses.
2. I am sure that these intruders are Pakistani soldiers. After winning the peak, don't start with the celebrations. The counter-attack of Pakistan comes swiftly, so be ready for that.
3. Don't behave like a superhero and expose yourself to the enemy. The strength of the troops lies with their

leader. The moment the leader dies, troops lose their confidence, and then no one will remain alive. The commander or leader has to live during the mission, and if he has to lay down his life, it should only be for the success of the mission.'

The CO responded to Subedar. 'Sahab, thank you so much. You are the most experienced soldier here. We will remember your points and act accordingly.'

All the officers smiled and shook hands with the Subedar and left to prepare for the climb.

The soldiers would receive their meals only once in a few days, yet, most of them left their food packets behind to make space for extra bullets and grenades. It was extremely tough to climb at the height of 13,000 feet in the freezing cold, and on windy nights. The low oxygen levels caused breathlessness, blood pressure dips and nose bleeds. While walking, they had to maintain utter silence and take every step consciously, looking out for land mines scattered intentionally by the enemy on the approaching paths. Any mistake could ruin the entire mission. Any moment could be the last moment of their lives as the enemy was watching from the height. Each soldier getting ready for the attack that night had the heart of a lion and the courage of an eagle. They stepped out from their shelters like it was their last day, and they had to place the Indian flag on Tololing peak at any cost.

At 6.30 pm, Capt. Akhilesh Saxena, with his FOO team, started executing massive artillery fire on the enemy bunkers on Tololing peak. He began with Bofors 155-mm guns, using the heavy guns in direct firing mode, targeting the enemy bunkers. Within minutes, the 105-mm guns followed, and then he ordered, 'Ten rounds gunfire'.

Immediately, 120 artillery guns simultaneously opened fire towards Tololing peak. It was night when the entire sky lit up with a bright golden-red glow that looked like millions of fireworks blooming, as he resorted to non-stop firing for several hours. Shell after shell slammed into the ridges. At the range of 35 km, it was very difficult to direct fire accurately, but there was no scope for mistakes. The experiment to use Bofors in a direct firing role appeared to be successful. The intruders ran into the bunkers to take cover, but the deadly salvo killed many of them. As expected, Pakistani counter bombardment began in retaliation.

Around 8.30 pm, the leading companies of 2 Rajputana Rifles started climbing in groups of just two or three at a time, from their assigned routes. The first soldier who moved up carried Karni Mata's picture around his neck. It was the belief of the soldiers that Karni Mata would protect them. Capt. Akhilesh began climbing up and kept directing the artillery fire on the enemy from a vantage point. The infantry troops felt confident enough with the artillery's expertise to cut down safety margins and take some risks. Capt. Akhilesh's job got tougher and required sharp accuracy as the Indian troops reached closer to the peak. He had to save his comrades and continued firing at the enemy bunker. When the troops reached near Tololing peak, he stopped firing the artillery guns as the enemy and our Indian troops were in the same location. The enemy now opened up with machine guns on the crawling Indian troops. Despite the continuous and threatening machine-gun fire from the enemy bunkers, Indian troops had to crawl towards it. They used grenades to silence them. With the battle cries, *Raja Ramchandra Ki Jai* and *Karni Mata Ki Jai,* all the officers and soldiers of the Indian Army charged with snipers, rifles and machine guns in hand. Finally, the troops approached and engaged in brutal hand-to-hand combat. Capt. Akhilesh saw a bayonet commando knife with an eight-inch blade as the enemy attacked him from the back and grabbed his neck, as though it were a cutaway shot of an old movie. In the illumination of explosion by the sides, a light ray reflected from the sharpened steel and blinded Capt. Akhilesh for a second. Convinced he was going to die, he didn't want to surrender without resistance. Knowing that he was going to be stabbed, he rolled on to his left shoulder and desperately kicked the enemy's face. Lunging forward, he brought the blade of the bayonet knife close to the enemy's neck and ripped at it, giving the man a deep gash through his neckline. His blood spouted out like a fountain and left Akhilesh's uniform wet. He froze for a few seconds after cutting the throat of an intruder. It was the first time he had killed someone, but within a moment, he snapped out of it. That was the moment where you either killed or got killed.

The Indian troops had a hard time fighting as the enemy was prepared with all forms of ammunition. Maj. Gupta kept his word, leading from the front. As he advanced, he stepped on a landmine that blew his foot. He stood up, limped forward and established his LMG gunner in position to fire at the enemy. At that moment, two enemy bullet shots brought Maj. Gupta down. The LMG gunner brought heavy fire on the enemy and sustained for a while. Soon, enemy grenades killed JCO Lal. By 2.30 a.m., dejection was setting in. Charged with anger, Havaldar Y.S. Tomar collected the grenades from the rest of the soldiers. He took an assault rifle in one hand and a grenade in the other, and attacked the last few bunkers. In the meantime, B Company reached the flat ridge of Tololing.

The radio set near Col Ravindranath buzzed, 'Cobra no more,' signalling that Maj. Gupta had died. There was no time for mourning. He directed Alpha Company to move forward, as per the plan.

Our soldiers observed that the front face of Tololing Top was filled with many small bunkers connected with sangar tunnels (paths created with rocks). Each bunker was loaded with ammunition, weapons and the space for a couple of intruders to hide. Tololing Top had huge concrete bunkers with ceilings constructed of heavy steel girders, and enormous boulders covering them. These bunkers were so secure that they could even be spared from rocket launchers. The enemy had been well-prepared by building powerful protection around them. It also reflected that they had been there long enough to have carried construction material with them. Amid chaos, smoke and gunfire, Indian soldiers took over the enemy bunkers. Indian officers and soldiers fought like undefeated warriors. Many intruders got killed, and many ran towards Point 5140. Our soldiers got into the bunkers and discovered the identity cards and documents that proved these intruders were official soldiers of the Pakistan Army. They also found many types of equipment such as splinter-proof jackets, powerful binoculars, night-vision devices and snow boots, which had never been privileged for Indian soldiers. By this time, Alpha Company reached Barbad Bunker. Finally, mad with anger, our soldiers killed the last two intruders captured in one bunker. Back at the base, the CO was huddling around the wireless. At 4.10 a.m., the news came crackling through – Tololing Top had been won! It was the first major victory of the Kargil War, and there was exultation all along the front. Every available camera captured the moment.

After hoisting the Indian flag on Tololing peak, the soldiers realized the extent of their injuries. There wasn't a single one of them not bleeding. The splinters of the enemy shelling had caused cuts through their combat uniforms. A few had survived but were in terrible shape with burns and severe injuries. Many lost limbs and were bleeding at the edge of death. They needed full medical attention immediately, but they were helpless and had to wait until the rescue team arrived. Everyone was weak, tired and hungry. They wanted to sit down and catch their breaths for a while, but they knew the job was not over. Indian troops now had to hold off the Pakistani counter-attack. The bodies of Maj. Adhikari and others were lying outside the bunkers where they had fallen around 17 days ago. The blood stains on the Indian uniform on the dead bodies brought tears to the eyes of every soldier standing by the side and saluting. With moist eyes, Capt. Akhilesh told the soldiers to arrange the bodies respectfully and cover them. As a soldier attempted to lift one of the bodies, an explosion from it shocked everyone. His leg blew up into the air, with muscle, pieces of tissue, bones and blood scattered all around. Blood began pooling on the sharp barren rocks from his slashed leg. He dropped on the rocks with a scream. Capt. Akhilesh was in shock for a few seconds before running to help his soldier. He was bleeding and crying in pain. A few others also rushed forward to help. They immediately fetched their field dressings, but the wound was too big. He was left with only one leg, and the other was lying a few metres away, lifeless.

A soldier shouted, 'Sir, these bastards have placed land mines in the bodies of our officers. They knew we would take the bodies to carry out their last rites.'

Another soldier yelled, 'I will behead them and cut their bodies into pieces.' He turned towards the body of the enemy lying at a distance. It's tough to stay calm in such situations, but officers cannot afford to lose their cool even for a minute. Capt. Akhilesh put his hand on the shoulder of his soldier and said, 'We are not butchers or devils; we are Indian soldiers. They have shown their character, and we will show ours. After death, they are not our enemies anymore. We are fighting for our country, and they fought for their country. We should always respect a soldier. Place the bodies of their men respectfully on one side. Scattered dead bodies and body parts all around don't evoke a sense of pride even in victory. But first, let us detect the landmines and clear the ground.' He then added, 'Those who still have some energy left, help your injured friends rest inside the bunker, which is possibly the only space on the peak without landmines.'

They found the entire front face of the peak filled with landmines. There was not even a square foot where the enemy hadn't planted landmines. Our soldiers were standing on ground that could blow apart with the slightest movement. Soldiers began clearing the landmines and helping their wounded comrades. They settled the wounded soldiers one by one inside the enemy bunkers, as it was the safest place, giving them hope that they would be rescued soon and their injuries attended to by a doctor.

Capt. Akhilesh stepped inside the bunker to motivate the injured soldiers. That sight is still alive as a jagged fragment of memory torn from the rest of the story, like a piece of shrapnel embedded forever in his mind. One soldier had lost both his legs and was bleeding profusely, another tried to press the bandage firmly with his palm to control the bleeding from his buddy's wounds but remained unsuccessful. The man sitting next to him was bleeding from the nose, ears and mouth. Another was sitting with just one hand. Another was bleeding from the eyes due to splinter injuries. One was bleeding from where a grenade had hit him in the stomach. One was bathed in blood, completely still. His buddy could only feel his pulse. There were around 35 soldiers bleeding who could succumb to death at any moment due to excessive blood loss.

'Just keep breathing, keep talking to each other, and don't lose consciousness. Our rescue team will arrive soon. Till then, please stay alive. It's an order.' Capt. Akhilesh himself was feeling nauseous but he had to stay strong.

A wounded soldier held his stomach and whispered, 'Sir, we are hungry and thirsty. There is nothing left to eat and no water to drink, as we carried grenades instead of food packets.'

Capt. Akhilesh heard him and observed that most of the snow on the ground had turned red with the blood of the fallen soldiers and black in some places, from blasts and gunpowder. There was not a single patch of clean snow to melt and satisfy the thirsty soldiers. He told another soldier, 'Look carefully. There must be a kitchen here. They were here for two months or longer, so they were definitely cooking and eating.'

Naik Shyamanand, with a few soldiers, inspected the location and reported. 'Sir, we can't find a kitchen here, but we can see a small bunker down in the valley towards the Pakistani side, between the ridges of two mountains.'

Capt. Akhilesh scrutinized it carefully, and said. 'I think that must be the kitchen. I will bring something to eat for everyone.'

Naik Shyamanand said, 'Sir, it is dangerous. That bunker is visible from the adjacent peak, and Pakistanis sitting on it will definitely open fire at you.'

'Perhaps, but if I succeed, we will at least not die because of hunger. It is downhill, and I will reach it within no time. You give me cover,' Capt. Akhilesh replied while loading his machine gun.

'I am coming with you, sir.' It was the voice of the youngest officer there. 'You won't be able to carry everything yourself, you need a hand.' He had come with Alpha Company, eager to support his comrades.

'Okay, let's go.'

Both the officers slung empty bags on their backs. One held a machine gun, and the other took some smoke bombs. And they ran downhill. The enemy sitting on the adjacent peak couldn't figure out why only two soldiers were running downhill. By the time they opened fire, both of them were inside the bunker.

The bunker was filled with dry fruit, packed food, honey and Karachi halwa.

'I think they were so sure of their victory that a party feast was prepared in advance.'

'They prepared food for the winners, and only winners will eat it.' Capt. Akhilesh smiled.

Both officers filled their bags with the food. Now it was difficult to climb up to the peak, as the enemy was alert, and their guns were targeting the bunker. Capt. Akhilesh used a smoke bomb and they began climbing uphill in the haze of smoke. The enemy was waiting for this moment, and opened fire on both of them. But our soldiers were covering both the officers, so they made it back to the bunker without getting hit by a single bullet. After distributing the eatables to everyone, they ate the most memorable meal of their lives.

As soon as the rescue team arrived, Capt. Akhilesh, along with the other officers and soldiers, rushed inside the bunker to help send the injured to the medical camp at the firm base. Some of the injured could not survive, leaving their disfigured and disabled bodies forever. The bunker was witness to the fact that eventually, death was not that painful. One statement from a fellow soldier brought streams of tears to everyone around. *Sahab zinda reh kar bhi kya karte, achcha hai shaheed ho gaye, aise shareer ke saath zindagi inhe har roz maar deti.*'(Sir, it's better that their souls left these disfigured bodies and they could become martyrs, or else they would have died every single day living disabled lives.)

Col Ravindranath reached Tololing peak, but many of his men who had invited him for breakfast were lying lifeless. He conveyed to the brigade commander on the radio set, 'Sir, I am on Tololing Top. My boys did it.' It was the first significant victory of the Indian Army after many failed attempts; it was a moment for rejoicing and celebration. A huge morale booster for the entire force. It became the turning point in the war. It was proven that nothing was impossible for Indian soldiers. But at the 2

Rajputana Rifles and 18 Grenadiers camps, mourning set in for the losses they had suffered. A total of four officers, two JCOs and seventeen OR were dead, and seventy wounded, of whom twenty-six were incapacitated and would never lead a normal life again. Col Ravindranath ordered, 'First take the injured and the bodies of the fallen officers of 18 Grenadiers to the base. Our martyred soldiers will be carried down later.' He then wept, leaving everyone in tears.

The following day, the news was flashed across newspapers and television channels that soldiers of the Indian Army had hoisted the tricolour on Tololing peak. I saw Akhilesh on television with the troops of 2 Rajputana Rifles after they captured Tololing peak and placed our national flag on it again. Everyone around me recognized a familiar face among the stained faces of our brave soldiers. The students of my centre surrounded me and shouted 'Jai Hind!', while tears rolled down my cheeks. Those who knew me, hugged me, while strangers saluted me and some even touched my feet. I felt very emotional and proud. That day, I understood that destiny had chosen to test my faith and courage. Marrying an army man is a firm commitment. It's not just the officers who are required to be brave, their wives must display courage too.

After two days, Dehradun mourned when the body of Maj. Gupta was brought to his hometown. A young officer of 28, wrapped in a flag, was lying dead in front of his father, himself a retired army officer. While a young lady in an Army Medical Corps officer's uniform, Rajshree, Maj. Gupta's wife, grieved silently for her husband who had died during the Kargil operation. Sobbing quietly, she saluted the man she had married in June 1997. It was a harrowing sight for everyone present. It brought tears to every eye and grief in every heart. There were several others besides friends and family; as for them, the man who died was not a stranger but a warrior who had sacrificed his life for their future. I arrived with my father, just in time for the funeral. It was the shared bond of the army uniform, the gruelling war and deep pain that drove me there. As I looked at Rajshree, I imagined myself in her situation. I could relate to her. This bitter incident could occur with me at any moment. It was tough to keep calm, but Rajshree did. I found her brave and dedicated to the nation. This young lady left me inspired and motivated to handle the challenges of being married to an army officer. She shook me out of depressing thoughts such as, *I would end my life if Akhilesh did not return from war.* It would be a cowardly deed and would defame his sacrifice. Rather than ending my life, I could dedicate it to the welfare of our soldiers and their families. I realized even if my husband died, my love for him would never fade, and I too love my country in the same way he does.

The news of the deaths of Maj. Adhikari and many more soldiers left everyone in a sombre mood. The bodies of our martyrs were returning to their families in coffins. I felt deeply saddened for them and visited their homes. As a member of the AWWA, it was my duty to offer my condolences to them. It was not an easy task at all. My heart sank each time I extended my arms to hug a mourning lady whose husband would never return home, and every time I placed my hands on the heads of innocent children unaware that they would never feel the warmth of their father's embrace again. I too cried with them. I was reminded of Akhilesh. He too was fighting in the same place that these fallen brave soldiers had returned from.

The environment was gloomy, but I didn't want to give up hope at any cost. My sleepless nights were spent in silent prayers for the war to end, looking at the flame of the lamp in front of the idol of Lord Vishnu placed next to the photograph of Akhilesh. Every moment, I asked God to take care of our soldiers.

THE HUMP

A soldier doesn't fight because he hates what's in front of him. He fights because he loves what he is fighting for.

The defeat of Tololing's peak was unbearable to the enemy. It had been their deepest penetration into Indian Territory and now, they had lost it. They were beginning to get restless, like a snake waiting to unleash its vengeance. Embittered by the loss of their forward-most outpost in Drass, the enemy kept pounding the Tololing ridgeline with heavy artillery fire from the adjacent peak of Hump, and Tololing was still vulnerable to a counter-attack. The Hump complex lay between Tololing and Point 5140, comprising around 10 high grounds numbered I to X on an equivalent ridgeline, each with a concrete enemy bunker scattered in a spine formation.

The victory of Tololing boosted the confidence of our troops. Still, men coming down the mountains carrying their dead and wounded comrades every night was a dreadful sight. Soldiers who were injured came down to the base camp, and those who were left with some energy took up position on the post to hold the success. The 2 Rajputana Rifles regiment moved downhill because of heavy casualties, and 18 Grenadiers was ordered to maintain the momentum of the attack and exploit the success to recapture the Hump. Capt. Akhilesh stayed back to provide artillery support to the troops moving in. He found some space in the ridge between two boulders. He somehow adjusted himself inside it. At the height of 17,000 feet above sea level, with freezing, windy nights and direct burning sunlight during the day, this was his new home for a few more days, until they had thrown every intruder out of our country – a home without a roof, walls, electricity, water or toilet. Our troops were sitting at the enemy's gunpoint. Their 'toilet' was a rope tied on a boulder that led towards the deep gorge. They had to relieve themselves by holding the rope and hanging into the gorge. That too, before dawn. Any movement in the daytime resulted in the enemy's prompt spotting and killing with sniper firing. One afternoon, a soldier could not help it, due to an upset stomach, and stood up to relieve himself. He got a direct sniper shot on his head and fell to his death into that very gorge. His buddies just clenched their teeth and pursed their lips to suppress their anger as they could not do anything. With moist eyes, they just prayed for the departed soul and cursed their helplessness.

The enemy still had the advantage of height. Replenishment of ammunition and food supplies was extremely challenging because of continuous enemy firing. There were no provisions for cooking, as the enemy would be able to detect smoke and fire, and that could turn into a target for artillery shelling. Our troops would receive sacks filled with puris and five kg of pickle once in a few days, in the darkness of night. Each soldier would get two puris and one spoon of pickle to survive on for the next few meals. There was no water available as most of the snow was covered in gunpowder or blood. Soldiers had to remove rocks to dig pure snow, which they had to melt or suck on to satisfy their thirst. Our soldiers' last food delivery on this ridge was on 11 June. Post that, there was no food or water till the capture of the entire Hump area. The enemy continued targeted artillery shelling to damage our post, shelter and confidence, but despite all odds, Indian soldiers, living on so little, achieved the impossible with their fierce determination.

Once again artillery officers created an infallible Fire Plan named 'Shatrunash' to conquer the entire Hump area and Point 5140. Charlie Company of the 18 Grenadiers took up the task to conquer the Hump under the leadership of Major Joy Dasgupta and artillery officer, Capt. Prodipto Goswami, as their FOO. Indian Artillery guns roared to support their infantry buddies. Firing and hastening to escape counter bombardment, they maintained a withering fire, and soldiers continued climbing forward. Now, bristling with anger at the loss of their comrades, the Grenadiers charged on until they reached the first bunker and silenced it. However, the attack was stalling under heavy casualties, and there were nine more bunkers. Each bunker was loaded with ammunition, with two or three intruders hiding inside. It was a rear-guard action fight, a typical characteristic of the enemy; they would leave two to three men to continue firing in every bunker to delay the capture. At this stage, two brave soldiers made the assault a success and saved the day. Havaldar Dashrath Lal Dubey and Havaldar Udham Singh from different companies jointly took a courageous decision. Both simultaneously attacked some of the bunkers and cleared them. However, Havaldar Singh died at the last bunker they attacked. His last words were, *Arey, Dashrath, goli lag gayee.* (I've been hit). Yet, soldiers drove the enemy out and cleared eight bunkers of the Hump by the following evening.

Indian troops captured an enormous amount of the enemy's weapons and ammunition, including rocket launchers and 81-mm mortars. The large pack of weapons, held only by regular forces, were captured from inside the bunkers. They also found some vital documents like ID-cards and ration books of the regular Pakistani army. This evidence again shattered the myth that these men who had intruded were militants; it was now certain that the Pakistani army had deceived India by capturing our forward posts. The enemy displayed their crookedness once again while running towards Pakistan; they ruined the food stock with gunpowder and set fire to it. Red-yellow flames, burning high, turned all the food into ashes. Our soldiers were left with empty stomachs, even after recapturing most of the bunkers of the Hump. Due to heavy casualties, lack of connectivity and food supplies, the 18 Grenadiers then moved down to the base.

Capt. Akhilesh took over the artillery Fire Plan of 'Shatrunash'. There were few maps and they were needed by every CO, 2IC, BC, GPO and FOO of the assault team, Akhilesh didn't receive adequate maps of the terrain. He sketched out the map on a blank paper by looking at the features and registered the target. This often happened in the war zone. The best available person was appointed for the assault without proper documentation or preparation. It was the need of the hour. No one questioned it or pointed it out. It was not about who got the credit; they all had to achieve the goal as a team. During war, soldiers and officers fill each other's positions and targets with no expectations in return. During the Kargil War, regiments from different locations came together and instantly formed a new team for the assault. Most of them were meeting for the first time; many didn't recognize each other even in action. Officers were not wearing their ranks, as they were involved in the planning, and that put them at higher risk. Only the soldiers who had been together for a while recognized their offices and fellow soldiers. Often, the officers and soldiers from other regiments remained unrecognized.

As an artillery FOO, Capt. Akhilesh and his team with Major Kasana as battery commander, were re-orbited with 13 JAK Rifles who were on a mission to capture Humps IX and X, Rocky Knob and Point 5140. Capt. Akhilesh met Lieutenant Colonel Y.K. Joshi, who in the middle of the war was promoted to the rank of lieutenant colonel and had to take over the command of his regiment as CO, as his commanding officer was evacuated due to medical injuries. With a grown beard and deep lines on his forehead, he looked worried, as he was suddenly shouldering the responsibility of the entire regiment. He was brave enough to handle that challenge at his young age. 'Akhilesh, I look forward to the same the artillery support from you as you had provided on Tololing Top. I hope for the best,' said Lt Col Joshi.

'Sir, I will do my best,' replied Capt. Akhilesh without delay.

It was a short meeting. Trust and dependability were the basis of teamwork. Each one knew their responsibility and was ready to lay down their life for the success of the mission.

The enemy sangars on these features were almost impenetrable to attack by missiles or rocket launchers.

Their positioning on the ground shielded them from artillery firing; these sangars were holding up the attack. Capt. Akhilesh observed the features constantly for 24 hours for the success of the Fire plan 'Shatrunash'. Without caring for his life, he moved around with his team to register the target and send the coordinates to the gun location. Soon, the 155-mm Bofors artillery guns were redeployed to target the enemy bunkers directly on the top.

The next morning, Capt. Akhilesh met Lieutenant Vikram Batra, who later rose to the rank of captain, arrived with 13 JAK rifles and his company to recapture Point 5140. This feature was about 1,500 metres north of Tololing on the same ridgeline.

'Good to see you, Vikram, with a high josh,' said Capt. Akhilesh, extending his hand.

'Good to see you, sir, after the significant victory at Tololing. You guys have made our way easy. Artillery is really helping us out. Or else this mountain warfare would be impossible to win,' said Lt Batra said while shaking his hand.

'Everyone is doing their bit. Every soldier knows how the minor battle fought by him will fit into the larger picture, and how the success of his fighting will influence the entire war. I am a minor piece to be fit into my country's victory,' replied Capt. Akhilesh.

'You are generous, sir. As an infantry person, this is the first time I've understood the role of artillery and gunners in the war. I respect and admire you for this,' Lt Batra said.

'So are you, Vikram. This is a game of trust. You trust that when you climb, I will direct the gun shelling precisely.

I trust my buddies at the gun site; they will drop the shell at the correct location and time. One mistake by anyone could ruin the game, and we will never get another chance. The only important thing here is the pride of our country. I may fall but I will not let the tiranga (tricolour) fall,' Capt. Akhilesh said.

'Right, sir, I have promised my family and friends that I will either come back after hosting the tricolour, or I will return wrapped in it, but I will come back for sure. I am not afraid of any bullet or shell. In fact, the bullet with my name on it has not been made yet,' Lt Batra said with a confident smile.

'May you shine with glory and become an inspiration to everyone. Your presence has filled the troops with josh,' Capt. Akhilesh said patting his junior buddy's back. 'Are you married?' he then asked.

'No, sir. I am lucky to have command over my life, I'm not married yet. That's another reason for my fearless attitude. But I have a girlfriend,' Lt Batra replied while laughing. 'What about you, sir?'

'I've recently been married. I left my new bride to come here and fulfil the commitment I made to myself at the time of the passing out ceremony. *The safety, honour and welfare of your country come first, always and every time. The honour, welfare and comfort of the men you command come next. Your own ease, comfort and safety come last, always and every time,*' said Capt. Akhilesh.

'And where is your wife's place in your promise?' asked Lt Batra.

'She is with me – my ease, comfort and safety – so her priority is the lowest,' Capt. Akhilesh replied with a heavy voice.

'Then, you must take care of yourself. May God bless you with a long life because if you go down in glory, two people will die at the same time,' Lt Batra said with a thoughtful look.

'Vikram, you take care too. Your girlfriend must be waiting for you. May God protect us all, but the fact is, no one knows what destiny has in store for us. But surely, India will win.'

'True, sir. We don't have a choice other than winning, and we will make it,'

'When do you have to launch an attack for 5140?' asked Capt. Akhilesh.

'After you clear Rocky Knob, it is around 800 metres away from 5140. It can provide us with the best avenue for mounting an attack.'

'We will clear bunkers IX and X of the Hump and Rocky Knob today itself,' Capt. Akhilesh said confidently.

'All the best, sir. I hope to win the feature with no casualties,' Lt Batra said.

'I will try my best to protect every soldier climbing towards the feature,' Capt. Akhilesh replied, while offering a silent prayer to the Almighty and closing his eyes.

The two of them waited together until the time of the assault, uncertain if they would ever meet again. The fact remained that in the chaos of war, they would never meet again. That day as well, the soldiers went hungry as there was no way food could be sent uphill. In the daytime, any movement would result in death by an enemy sniper shot and nights were reserved for assaults, so there was no time for food.

Capt. Akhilesh started executing artillery firing on the top of the Hump with his radio operating team. The faith of infantry battalion in the direct artillery firing was so complete that they pressed home their attack during daytime. Major S. Vijaya Bhaskar, who was leading the Alpha Company of 13 JAK Rifles started climbing up for the assault. Once again, the Bofors guns took a heavy clang. Akhilesh directed artillery firing, one after another, without a delay bang on the enemy bunkers. The sound of the shelling thundered through the valley, and the smell of the explosion permeated every breath present. The enemy began running away from the sangar in an attempt to save their lives. Eight enemy soldiers were killed, and many more were injured by the heavy artillery fire. 13 JAK Rifles conquered Humps IX and X and Rocky Knob with no Indian casualties. The brigade received the message that the entire area of the Hump and Rocky Knob was now under the possession of the Indian Army. Now, they could move towards capturing Point 5140.

The injured soldiers moved down to the base. From Capt. Akhilesh's team, Naik Dashrath had to leave as he was bleeding profoundly from his nose. The rest of the assault team held the area until 18 June, when the next lot of Indian troops from the base arrived with reinforcements. Indian soldiers were busy clearing the landmines from the path of the troops about to march forward for the attack on Point 5140. Suddenly, Capt. Akhilesh's radio set buzzed, 'Dogs, you have come too far. Go back or else none of you will remain alive. I have come from Afghanistan where I specialized in beheading humans. If you come before me, I will cut your throats and hang your heads on the boulders. Save your lives, go back home.' Our frequency had gotten connected to the enemy but the soldiers were used to it by now. Instead of being frightened, driver R. Gwate shouted, 'We have made you run like dogs from every place you were hiding in. It would be better for you all to leave our country or else, we will send you to hell. Bastard!' Everyone burst into laughter as he was the tiniest among them. Capt. Akhilesh smiled and switched off the radio set for a while.

On the night of 18 June, 13 JAK Rifles from the south, 18 Garhwal Rifles from the east, and 1 Naga from the southwest made an assault for Point 5140. The brigade planned a multidirectional assault because of the enormous size of the feature. All the divisional artillery and infantry motors available in the Drass sector came into action. Artillery thunder shelling vibrated through the entire ridge again. By the morning of 20 June, Indian soldiers had cleared all the sangars and forced the Pakistanis to run back towards their own country. Lt Batra conveyed his success signal to his CO, '*Yeh dil maange more* (The heart wants more).' This message echoed across Indian news channels, and the expression of josh filled the heart of every citizen. This was the advertising slogan of a popular soft drink, but from that day onwards, Indians associated it with the mark of victory expressed by braveheart Lt Batra.

Capt. Akhilesh and his radio operating team came down to Drass after the success of Hump and moved to his regiment location at Draupadi Kund. After two continuous assaults and 14 days on the harsh and inhuman battlefront, they needed to rest and recuperate. His handsome face was almost hidden by a long beard. He had lost around 18 kg and was turning weak, due to lack of nutrition and sleep.

The merciless cold weather impacted him deeply; his skin had turned extremely dry and black, his lips were filled with cuts. He desperately wanted to take a bath, shave and wear clean clothes, but warm water wasn't available, and a shower with cold water would freeze him. Like Aladdin's genie, his buddy somehow arranged for some warm water, but because of the weather, it turned cold within a few minutes. Somehow, he managed to take a bath and clean the filth of 14 days. His helper then brought him a mug of hot tea as he sat outside his tent. Capt. Akhilesh took the mug, raised it to himself in a toast, and wrapped his fingers around it to feel the warmth. The aroma of the tea brought back memories of the evening teapot Shikha used to serve him, along with cheese balls. Once, he burned his mouth with the melted cheese and Shikha apologized for serving them so hot. And he just smiled, pulled her towards him and kissed her. Breathing deeply, he kept watching the spectacular display of the stars. As he closed his eyes, the image of Shikha appeared in front of him. He wanted to hold her tight, kiss her gently, smell her deeply and love her passionately. He didn't want to check the platoon's guns and weapons. He just wanted something cosy to lie upon and sleep for a long time. But with darkness coming on, there was no time to relax. He was assigned other operational responsibilities, as his big guns were continuously firing and supporting various other infantry attacks.

The next day, they received a huge jute sack filled with letters. Everyone was expecting one from back home. Havaldar Kashavlal called out names and started handing over the letters. Each soldier was reading his letter with a smile and moist eyes. A couple of packages had arrived too late as their recipients were no more. Akhilesh received a bunch of letters and cards that I'd written to him daily; they had all arrived together. As he read each letter over and over, his shed little teardrops and smiled as well. He held the letters close to his heart and kissed them just as he was yearning to hug and kiss Shikha. As he continued lying on his sleeping bag with the letters and cards spread all over, Havaldar Kashavlal visited him.

'*Sahib, kuchh khat aise hain jo khaas hain. Kripaya unhen zor se padhen jab main sabhi ko ikatha karoon* (Sir, there are a few special letters. Please read those aloud when I get everyone assembled),' he requested.

In the evening, Havaldar Kashavlal gathered everyone outside the kitchen tent, and Capt. Akhilesh read the letters out loud.

The first letter was written in blood. 'Brothers, I salute you all. We are protected only because you are standing between us and the enemy. My grandfather had witnessed the partition of India. It was horrible and terrifying; demons in human form raped women and girls on the streets, slashed the throats of young boys and old men and left them lying in pools of blood. There were dead bodies on every lane, in every house or shop. We are afraid it may happen again. But we trust you and pray for your success. I wanted to join the Indian army but could not clear the entrance tests. I am writing this letter with my blood, to express my respect to you all. Don't let the enemy reach our houses. Fight for your sisters and mothers. Jai Hind.'

Akhilesh touched the words inked in blood and shouted, 'Even at the cost of our lives, we will never let the enemy enter our country. The honour and respect of our women will be protected at any cost.'

'Ji Sahab, We will fight until our last breath. Jai Hind!' everyone shouted together.

The second letter was a package containing several rakhis (amulets tied by sisters around the wrists of their brothers, on the festival of Raksha Bandhan, to symbolize protection) and a letter. 'I am the widow of Sepoy Kuldeep Singh. I lost my husband in the war of 1971. My daughters were five and eight when the body of their father was brought to our village. I was young and found myself all alone in the crowd of relatives. Life didn't stop, but it is not the same. I consider all of you my brothers. We villagers conduct puja every evening at our village temple, praying for your lives. We are sending rakhis for all of you. You are our saviours and our protectors. May God protect you and bring you back home to your families soon.'

After reading the letter, Akhilesh took a deep breath, and said, 'People are conducting pujas for our lives. They have faith that we will win and protect them. We have to uphold their faith in us.'

'Sahab, we will not disappoint them. Whether we return to our homes or not, one thing is for sure, we won't let the enemy inside the houses of our countrymen. They are our people, our responsibility,' Havaldar Kashavlal said as everyone agreed, 'Ji Sahab Ji'.

The letters were like a motivational dose, and the soldiers were filled with new energy as they resumed their duties.

The next day, some news reporters, including Barkha Dutt, interviewed Capt. Akhilesh. He enthusiastically explained the role of artillery guns and the FOO in the war. He told them about the major victories of the Indian Army, followed by a string of successes with the realization that we could beat the Pakistanis despite the odds. My students and I watched him live on TV, and everyone including the other staff members jumped with joy. 'Jai Hind!' echoed through the air and not only at the reception area, but outside the institute too. I smiled after many days, but I had tears in my eyes too. Akhilesh looked weak, and the impact of the harsh weather was evident on his face.

After the interview, he requested Barkha to lend him the satellite phone so he could speak to his wife.

'Sir, please don't embarrass us. You are doing so much for our country. This is the least we can do for you,' Barkha smiled and connected her satellite phone to the number Capt. Akhilesh gave her.

A long ring on the landline phone in the office of Arena Multimedia signalled that this call was for me. I immediately picked up the receiver. 'Hi, I am Shikha speaking,' I said, with no delay.

'Hi! Honey, I miss you a lot. Just listen to me carefully. This is a satellite phone. Only one person can speak at a time. I don't know when I will be able to speak to you again,' he explained.

'I am listening,' I responded.

'I am so in love with you that I can't imagine my life without you, and I know it is the same for you, but you are married to an army officer. Even if I am not with you, you must continue to smile. Do you understand what I mean?' He was hesitating to convey his insecurity to me.

'Yes, I understand what you want to say.' Tears started flowing from my eyes.

'I am not sure when we will meet again, but I am sure you will always be proud of me.' His voice was losing strength.

'I am proud of you. Not just me, everyone is proud of you, and you will come back. Don't even think about not coming back. You have to stay alive to keep contributing to the nation. *Tum bas josh me hosh nahi khona* (Just don't lose your cool). Don't worry about me and focus on your work. I have complete faith in God. Everything will be all right soon.' I was no longer able to control my emotions.

'I love you, honey. You don't worry too. I will come back for you,' he assured me. And in my heart, I knew he had given me his word.

I knew, on the other side, he too was smiling with tears in his eyes. Our pain and duty were of the same colour, only his was a shade darker. He was living in such harsh conditions, that it brought tears to my eyes just trying to imagine it. More than love, respect was now gripping my heart for Akhilesh. In my prayers, I often bargained with God to add years to Akhilesh's life and subtract them from mine.

THREE PIMPLES AREA

War is not just the shower of bullets and
bombs from both sides,
It is also the shower of blood and bones on both sides.

It was the night of 26 June 1999. Raucous sounds of bombardment echoed across the Valley. The Drass village went under a thick layer of smoke and fire, with the frustrated enemy indulging in targeted shelling on it from the Pakistan side. The silent, empty cottages with no human traces were burned down to ashes. The Indian Army had made the proactive decision of moving the villagers to a safer place, providing food and shelter to them before this incident. Apart from the Indian troops, only a few villagers witnessed this rain of fire. They had stayed back willingly to support the soldiers, as they were familiar with the terrain. Eyes moist and in helplessness, they witnessed their houses burning. Their only hope now was for the Indian troops to recapture all the mountain peaks so there would be peace, and they could rebuild their homes. Capt. Akhilesh also observed this ruthless artillery shelling of the enemy from a short distance. He and his FOO team were associated with the 2 Rajputana Rifles once again, as the soldiers demanded the same artillery officer who supported them in breaking the stalemate against the enemy and emerging victorious at Tololing. They were confident of repeating the action and conquering the Three Pimples Area with him.

Capturing Three Pimples as soon as possible was crucial, as it was another feature dominating the national highway, Drass village and Sando nala. From here, the enemy minutely observed the movement of Indian troops and pointed artillery fire at them. This area is a cluster of sharp, commanding mountaintops near Point 5100 on the Marpo La ridgeline, west of Tololing nala. This complex comprises three features: Knoll, Lone Hill and Three Pimples. The 2 Rajputana Rifles regiment had set up their firm base near this complex at the steep slope of the ridge. The artillery fire of Pakistan could not reach this location as it was not within their parabolic range. Planning an attack was an arduous task, with the days rapidly moving towards the full-moon night. It would favour the enemy, as our movements would be visible to them from the peaks they were sitting upon. To wait for the pitch darkness of night meant losing another 15 days, and this could give the enemy time to reinforce their ammunition, men and weapons.

It had been just a week since Capt. Akhilesh had gone down to the base camp and he was called for another attack. Minor sprains, cuts and injuries could not keep this daredevil away from war action. He was still on a mission to drag the enemy out of our LOC. This was his third attack, accompanied by Naik Charlis and radio operator Naik Suresh Chand Singh as his FOO team. Major Ashok Sharma joined Capt. Akhilesh as his battery commander to execute artillery Fire Plan 'Agnibaan'. They developed a strong bond while sharing the uncertainty of life and planning for the success of the mission. These two gunners took the responsibility of clearing the uphill path for their infantry buddies and blowing out the enemy bunkers before our soldiers reached the peak. Akhilesh would climb with leading troops and Maj. Sharma would coordinate from the base. They tested Fire Plan, but the target was not in direct range this time. They plotted 20-fire units (about 120 guns), including Bofors, 155-mm medium guns, motors and rocket launchers. And they positioned Bofors in place to fire directly at the targets. The aim was to bombard the enemy bunkers with high-power artillery shells and explosives.

To ensure the success of 'Agnibaan' Capt. Akhilesh, along with his team, was awake in the middle of the night, observing the Three Pimples area in detail and registering the accurate coordinates of the enemy position to direct massive artillery fire at their bunkers. There was no scope for an error. He marked all the three features – Knoll, Lone Hill and Three Pimples – on the grid lines of the map in hand, but the feature was widespread. This time he had to direct fire on all the three features while simultaneously providing cover to all the leading infantry troops. Every attack was unique, and he prepared for distinct challenges each time. They ranged and directed three to four shots of shelling on the three targets and pinpointed the exact locations on the map, noting the accurate coordinates. This time, the concern was the moonlight and cold wind, which began blowing from the north to the east, especially during nights. It could change the coordinates.

All the officers had a meeting with the CO on 28th morning. Alpha Company would approach Knoll under the leadership of Maj. Acharya, accompanied by Capt. Thapar. Bravo Company would assist Alpha Company in a counter-attack and target Three Pimples. Capt. Akhilesh would direct artillery fire on the entire ridge as lead FOO and Maj. Saxena would help Delta Company approach Lone Hill. Capt. Kengurüse, Ghatak Platoon Commander, would assist Delta Company.

The regiment was ready with an action plan for assault, but the enemy's movements were unknown. The glowing brightness of the moon was now a point of concern in everyone's mind, but no one uttered a word. There was silence among the soldiers. A deep melancholy taking possession of the regiment was clear from the soldiers' faces. The entire nation was looking at them to redeem the prestige of the country. So, they decided to achieve victory, even at the cost of their lives. Every soldier of the regiment was ready to sacrifice his life for the pride of his unit.

Col Ravindranath sensed the anxiety under the carpet of silence. He called his key members for a meeting after lunch, and said, '*Paltan ki izzat aaj aapke hatho me hai* (The honour of the regiment is in your hands now). Rajputana Rifles has had a golden history in military warfare. We have never lost our courage under any circumstance. You all are like my sons. Being a father, I just want to say, it is the need of this hour to sacrifice oneself. We need to fight until our last breaths. We need to fight until we conquer. Fight like lions and drag them out of our country. I know it is difficult, which is why the Indian Army has chosen Rajputana Rifles. They have trusted us, and we will not let them down.'

'Sahab, we will win, or we will not come back. *Ham apne paltan ki izzat girne nahi denge,*' said a subedar.

'Ji, Sahab, don't worry. One more event of history will sing the saga of Rajputana Rifles,' said another.

'We will walk in front of you. I will take the first bullet. But promise me, even if I fall, you will not stop until we place the tricolour on the peak of Three Pimples,' Maj. Acharya told his troops.

'*Sahab aap ko kuchh nahi hoga*,' said a soldier. 'We will win and put our national flag on the peak by morning.'

'*Raja Ramchandra ki jai, Karni Mata ki jai!*' they all said as they raised their right hands in the air with closed fists to symbolize their dedication to do or die. With this, everyone dispersed to prepare for the assault.

Maj. Acharya, Capt. Akhilesh, and Capt. Thapar were sitting together on a boulder when Capt. Thapar broke the silence with an ominous tone in his voice. 'Sir, we have prepared the soldiers for the fight but somehow, I think tonight is not a good time for the attack. I can see my death today.'

'Vijayant, never approach a fight with this mindset. I am with you, and they will have to kill me before getting to you,' Maj. Acharya said while placing his hand on Capt. Thapar's shoulder.

'Don't worry. Our fire plan is better than the one at Tololing. We will destroy the enemy bunkers before our boys get there,' said Capt. Akhilesh.

'The enemy could observe our movement in the moonlight and aim effortlessly,' said Capt. Thapar.

'Yes, they can,' Capt. Akhilesh said. 'During the early hours of the morning, well before dawn, I woke up from a terrifying dream in which I was falling... feeling as if the earth was slipping beneath me. I had lost my footing on the hill and was skidding towards the drop below, picking up speed while dragging my wife and parents with me on a rope. Before hitting the rock, my eyes opened abruptly in the darkness, and there was a hollow, hopeless feeling in my chest. For several minutes, I shivered in the cold. At that moment, I felt sure I was going to die. Never before had I experienced such complete helplessness.' After a pause, he added, 'But I am not going to give up. I will do my best.'

'How the movements will take place, no one knows. Just focus on your task and leave rest to God,' said Maj. Acharya.

'I'm relieved knowing that my brother, Birdy, will be around to take care of my parents. I just wish I had more time to spend with Naina,' Capt. Thapar said.

'My promise to share my life with Shikha seems to have ended too soon. How will she live without me? I know she will break down,' Capt. Akhilesh said in a broken voice.

'I too wish to take care of my pregnant wife and play with my child. But we must continue performing our duties,' Maj. Acharya advised them.

Both youngsters were listening to their senior and trying to follow the guidance of the Bhagavad Gita. Certain moments in life are beyond our reach, and we must follow the path without thinking about the destination. Only time will reveal what's in store for us. They then dispersed to write the last words they wished to convey to their loved ones. The imagination of death can leave anyone feeling hopeless. Each word written in the final letters by soldiers from the battlefront, communicates the pain and suffering they go through during these moments; writing as though they haven't made it back from the assault; writing to parents, wives, children; writing that they will never return home. Capt. Akhilesh was in tears as he wrote his final letters for the third time, to his parents and wife. These are the most vulnerable moments experienced by soldiers; they get nostalgic and emotional, feel depressed and cry too. Before facing the enemy, they must first fight their own emotions. Eventually, they gather the courage to fight, and lay down their lives for their country without a second thought. They are not superheroes, but genuine heroes. Capt. Akhilesh wrote his letters, sealed them and placed them in his bag. The army would send the bag to his parents and wife, in case he did not return.

Around 6 p.m., the regiment gathered to perform a puja to Karni Mata as they did before every assault to keep their faith high, fight with bravery and achieve victory. The troops then got ready for the assault, painting their faces black to merge into the darkness of night. But 28 June 1999 was a full-moon night. They tied kesariya banas on their heads, under their helmets, with a promise to return victorious. Suddenly, an airburst of concentrated artillery shelling from the enemy descended upon them, dropping thousands of splinters from the sky, and pierced the bodies of our soldiers like knives. Out of pure reflex, some of the soldiers sought shelter under the rocky cliff to save themselves from being blown to bits, but many were severely wounded before the assault even began. It was a terrifying setback; the enemy was aware of their firm base location.

'The enemy knows our location. We must leave immediately, or we will die here itself,' shouted the Subedar Major. 'Watch out for landmines, they must have planted them along the way. Take your steps cautiously.'

Naturally, the troops were now bewildered. Able soldiers supported the wounded ones and carried them to the medical camp. They had to leave their buddies behind in blood-soaked uniforms, and leave for their final assault on the enemy. The brave soldiers of Rajputana Rifles began climbing to defeat death that night, which they could see on the peaks. But they were not going to go down without fighting. All the four companies were making their way uphill through the nala from different directions, unaware of each other's positions. They were connected with a wireless set but avoided communication, as the enemy could intercept it and determine the direction of assault.

Capt. Akhilesh felt the pressure of having to save his infantry buddies from the enemy, who were waiting for them to come into their range of fire. He immediately directed artillery firing to begin, as he climbed uphill with Delta Company and Maj. Saxena towards Lone Hill. Once again, artillery made its presence felt, and accurate fire direction by Capt. Akhilesh helped the infantry make their way uphill. Once again, the Valley witnessed the massive explosions by the Indian artillery. The sky turned red and the air was thick with smoke. Offended by their defeat at Tololing, the enemy continuously bombed and fired from the top. As per the plan, Alpha Company, under the leadership of Maj. Acharya and Capt. Thapar, approached Knoll. And Bravo Company headed towards Three Pimples. Capt. Akhilesh was continually directing high-explosive artillery firing at the targets. Without a delay of even a second, he was smashing fireballs on the enemy bunkers. This kept the enemy with their heads hidden in the bunkers. The unknown and rugged terrain also became the cause of Indian casualties, which resulted in slow movement and prolonged exposure to enemy weapons. Our soldiers climbed for seven hours to reach the enemy amid the shower of bullets and bombs. It was no longer a game of hide-and-seek. The soldiers knew the enemy was watching in the moonlight. Now, it was just a matter of courage and reflexes.

The leading platoon of Alpha Company pressed on ahead and got into face-to-face combat with the enemy. Maj. Acharya kept his word and led from the front. A grenade hit his chest, leaving him in a pool of blood as his AK-47 dropped to the ground. He fell to his death, but his troops remained focused and continued fighting the enemy. Capt. Thapar, with a section of the troops a few miles behind, observed the firing. They quickly began moving towards the action. Soon, they too were part of the combat at Knoll. When Capt. Thapar found out about Maj. Acharya's martyrdom, he could not stop himself from charging the attack. He aimed at the enemy and started firing. At the same time, an enemy sniper aimed at Capt. Thapar and shot him straight in the face, snuffing the life out of the brave officer. Disturbed and weeping, but still undefeated, the soldiers of Alpha Company, despite the loss of their officers, stood courageous and maintained their position. Soon Bravo Company linked up with them to establish a foothold on Knoll.

In the meantime, in the purple glow of night, Delta Company, under the leadership of Maj. Saxena and Capt. Akhilesh, was advancing quietly towards Lone Hill. Capt. Akhilesh continually gave fire direction to the artillery guns to give cover to all the leading troops. With close-range observation of Three Pimples now available, with accurate artillery firing he aimed to quickly reduce the enemy to dust. Lone Hill was a commanding feature with a steep cliff face covered by enemy MMGs. The chilly air was cutting the exposed skin of the soldiers seeking their way through the rough and scattered boulders. It was obvious from the enemy's continuous firing and artillery shelling that they had sensed our action. There was not a single tree to take cover behind. Bomb shelling was falling very close, and it was just a matter of time when it could directly hit anyone. Escaping death under enemy fire, our troops were continuously dodging to avoid stepping on any landmines. They managed their way through the slippery route with minor casualties.

Now, troops reached the place from where they had to climb over a 200-feet high vertical rock. Capt. Kengurüse mounted the sheer rock face barefoot, literally hanging on by his fingers and toes. Soon, the Ghatak Commando Platoon scaled the cliff with perfection. The utter silence maintained by our soldiers broke as they reached the top of the cliff, and charged towards the enemy with the war cries, *'Karni Mata Ki Jai'* and *'Raja Ramchandra Ki Jai'*. They came under intense mortar, rocket launcher and automatic fire, which caused heavy casualties. The sound of machine guns and grenades penetrated the valley, and the cloud of smoke covered the peak. Capt. Kengurüse fought like a daredevil and killed two enemy soldiers, and then two more with his commando knife, but a grenade left him fatally wounded.

From the other side Capt Akhilesh was moving with his team and saw an enemy shell coming their way. 'Bend down,' he shouted and tried to push Naik Suresh down. They both dropped and took cover behind a boulder. Akhilesh felt a burning sensation in his left palm. He raised his hand to see if he was alright. He was shocked to find half his palm missing. All he could see was blood pouring out of his hand. Instinctively, he touched the wound with his right hand and felt the warmth of the blood. There were no muscles, tissues or bones left on half his palm. But there was no pain either; perhaps due to the cold. All he could feel was numb and damp skin. His fingers probed inside the gash for a second or two until he drew back, realising the severity. Blood streamed out and wet his entire arm. He somehow held his left wrist with his right palm and tried to pull out the field dressing with his teeth from the right chest pocket of his combat uniform. The blood made his grip slippery. He made several unsuccessful attempts to take the dressing out of his pocket till Naik Suresh and Naik Charlis by his side noticed him.

'*Sahab, aap ke haath se khoon beh raha hai* (Sir, your hand is bleeding),' Naik Suresh pointed out. 'It's nothing, you don't worry, I will manage.' Capt. Akhilesh told him. Naik Charlis helped Capt. Akhilesh retrieve the field dressing to dress the wound, but it seemed to be in vain. Blood was spouting out like a fountain. Capt. Akhilesh gathered his thoughts to stay calm and stood up, as he didn't want to lose focus on the target at the last hour. Without any further delay, he re-joined the troops in the combat fight.

After a while, Capt. Akhilesh's combat shirt got wet from the blood flowing out of his hand. It was only due to his mental strength that he didn't give up. He had to stay alive to fight for and protect his nation. But the soldiers realized that their officer was severely injured.

'*Sahab, ab hum sambhal lenge. Dushman marega ya fasega* (Sir, we will handle the situation. The enemy will either surrender or die, it's just a matter of time),' said a Rifleman of Rajputana Rifles.

'*Main theek hoon* (I am okay),' Capt. Akhilesh assured him, his sight blurring and voice trembling.

'Sahab, kasam se hum dushman par havi hai. Aap mar jaoge agar ye khoon nahi ruka (Sir, I promise we are in a dominating position. You will die if you continue bleeding),' Naik Charlis urged him.

'I will stay,' Akhilesh insisted again, but his condition was getting worse.

'Sahab, aapne apna kaam kar diya, ab hame karna hai. Aap ko medical base jaana chahiye (Sir, you have done your bit, now it is our turn. You should go to the medical base now),' one Rifleman of Rajputana Rifles said. He then turned to radio operator Suresh and instructed him, '*Sahab ko medial base pahuncha do* (Take sir to the medical base).'

Capt. Akhilesh realized he was losing consciousness. 'Okay, I will go, but I don't require anyone with me. I will walk down alone.'

'Sahab, main aap ke saath aya hoon, saath hi jaunga, (Sir, I've come with you, and I will return with you),' Suresh insisted.

Capt. Akhilesh was bleeding profusely. Charlis tied his officer's hand to his head to control the flow of blood. Capt. Akhilesh started walking downhill with Suresh.

The fight lasted for a few more hours, and eventually the Indian troops captured Lone Hill.

The handset buzzed with the declaration: 'Alpha calling Delta. We have captured Knoll and Three Pimples.' The reply was a victory message too: 'Delta is now on the top of Lone Hill. We too have captured the feature.' The dried up lips and black faces of the soldiers broke into huge smiles. They hugged each other and started crying. The tears flowed out with the mixed emotions of victory and loss; the precious loss of lives of their brothers who fought the brave fight to the end, and were still lying where they had breathed their last. The 2 Rajputana Rifles regiment had successfully captured the well-entrenched position of the enemy on the Three Pimples Area. They found a massive stockpile of ammunition and food rations inside the bunkers. The radio set at Headquarters beeped and announced the capture of Three Pimples. The news of the martyrdom of Maj. Acharya, Capt. Thapar, and Capt. Kengurüse left Col Ravindranath in tears. Headquarters sent immediate orders to enforce the troops for the Three Pimples Area.

Watan ki raah pe watan ke naujawan shaheed ho.

THE LAST SURVIVAL

You have never lived until you have almost died, and for those who choose to fight, life has a special flavour; the protected will never know.

The temperature was -18 degrees centigrade at the height of 16,000 feet in the war zone of Three Pimples, Kargil. It was midnight on 29 June 1999, and one's sight could travel for miles as there were no obstacles in view. The freezing cold, icy peaks of Kargil were shining like silver in the moonlight, offering visibility even in the dark cerulean glow. The thunder of heavy artillery shelling guns continued to shake the mountains. The golden fireballs of explosion turned everything into ash, wherever they dropped. The smell of gunpowder was dense in the air. The lack of oxygen had made breathing even more difficult. In the shower of fire, Capt. Akhilesh trudged downhill along with his radio operator. In the mountains, the trail is never straight. They were in the middle of a widespread rocky surface. Unaware of the correct direction, every step they took towards the medical camp was a gamble. They set out with measured strides, their inner compasses fixed on invisible coordinates that led them towards the nearest medical post. Both looked terribly exhausted with dirty, black faces and chapped lips. Their ragged uniforms appeared as though they had been dragged in the mud, and were torn from the sniper cuts on their bodies. The patches of blood stains on them were still fresh. Capt. Akhilesh's hand was tied to his head with a small bandage, while blood continued to trickle down his face, soaking his uniform. He was severely injured, and his hand was bleeding profusely. Each falling drop of blood was depleting him of energy. He was aware that most soldiers lose their lives due to blood loss from severe injuries. Despite being in a critical condition, he had conviction in his heart and a smile on his face. He was sure he could live up to the reputation of his uniform, serve his country and fulfil his assigned task. Even after being hit by splinters from the enemy's artillery shelling, he had hid his injury and continued fighting.

After four hours of their journey downhill, they were still quite a distance away from their destination. Capt. Akhilesh's eyes were getting heavier with each passing minute. As he walked with trembling legs, his right foot got stuck in a gap between two rocks. He tried to take another step but lost his balance and fell hard on the rocky surface, getting another cut on his face. Naik Suresh instantly turned around and pulled his leg out, and then assisted him in standing up. They resumed their journey as Capt. Akhilesh murmured, 'I have to live'. He remembered the words, *Stay alive to keep contributing to the nation.* The image of Shikha appeared in his thoughts, waiting at the railway platform, where he had seen her last. He was struggling to breathe and remain conscious, as the continuous bleeding threatened to draw him closer towards death. After they had covered a little more distance, his vision got blurry and his legs lost strength; breathing heavily, he fell to the ground and lost consciousness.

'*Sahab, aankhen kholo* (Sir, please open your eyes),' cried Suresh while sprinkling water on Capt. Akhilesh's face. He shook him repeatedly, holding his shoulders and slapping his face, but he got no response. The chances of saving him seemed near impossible.

After a few minutes, which felt like an hour, Capt. Akhilesh slowly opened his eyes. His vision was blurry and his eyes were red. An inner voice compelled him to open his eyes. He whispered, 'I can't die. I have to live.' He fought the enemy for his country and now, he had to gather all his strength to stand up and fight death for the love he had left behind. With trembling legs, he stood up and began waking again. There was a heaviness in his legs, but he continued to walk. By now, the first rays of sunlight had touched the top of the ridge.

Suresh pulled Capt. Akhilesh's right hand towards his shoulder and supported him, as they continued plodding downhill. Rough and slippery boulders along the way made their task difficult, and they tripped a few times. It was the longest and toughest journey he had ever been on, but giving up for even a single moment could have cost him his life. After several hours of walking, Capt. Akhilesh saw the medical post at a distance with his blurry vision, which soon turned into total darkness. He dropped to the ground. Waving both hands in the air, Singh ran to get help. The soldiers at the base camp were alert and motioned him to come closer on gun point. When they realized it was one of their men, they rushed to fetch a stretcher from the medical tent.

Maj. Ashok Sharma rushed to attend to his gunner officer. He tried to comfort him and stayed there till Capt. Akhilesh got his initial medical treatment. As soon as Col Ravindranath received the message, he called Dr Captain Somnath Basu. His mournful voice revealed his emotional turmoil. The tricolour was flying at the top of Three Pimples now. They had won, but paid a heavy price for it. Since that morning, he had cried over the loss of three young officers and eight ORs, while fifty-two others were wounded. Many had lost their ability to see, hear, walk or hold things forever. They would always live disabled lives.

'Doctor, I have seen enough of my men die. Please save him. I don't want to lose another life,' begged Col Ravidranath.

'Sir, I have dressed his wounds. He is still alive, but in critical condition because of the heavy blood loss. I can't say whether or not he will survive. We have requested for a chopper to take him to the 92 Base Hospital in Srinagar as soon as possible. I will send Capt. Akhilesh to the Gumari field medical base to meet the chopper. You proceed towards the peak as your soldiers are waiting for you,' Dr Capt. Basu said.

After the first dressing, Capt. Akhilesh was carried to the Gumari field medical camp on a stretcher. It was at a distance of one hour from the base medical camp. He was still bleeding, so the team of doctors performed the first surgery right there to stop the bleeding. The chopper arrived at the Gumari field medical base to airlift all the wounded soldiers on life support and carry them to the army base hospital in Srinagar; their last hope for survival.

At 92 Base Hospital, Srinagar, army doctors began working with patience and precision; checking Capt.

Akhilesh's injuries one by one. He had one major wound and dozens of minor cuts and bruises. Due to the cuts from the splinters, his wounds were filled with poisonous gunpowder. While trekking downhill, he had fallen on the rocks several times, so there was mud and gravel in the wounds. These had to be flushed out and disinfected before being stitched up. Before cleaning his wounds, the doctor bowed his head and prayed, along with all his assistants. Repairing the torn tendons and bones was a slow process that took hours. Meanwhile, Capt. Akhilesh was given several units of blood and a steady drip of saline solution.

He remained unconscious and under critical observation in the ICU for one day. Doctors were not sure about his survival. On 1 July, he opened his eyes, but he was too weak to speak. They moved him to the general ward and kept him under observation for one more day. Every rising sun infused some energy into him, and he began to feel slightly better. When he opened his eyes, he noticed his entire left hand under temporary plaster, scratches and bandages on his legs, and a terrible pain in his back. His left leg had been cut to the bone and the tendons severed, but he had no recollection of this injury. His body movements were restricted and only his right hand was free to move. He gestured to the nurse to come closer as he could barely speak.

'I want to speak to my wife. May I?' he muttered.

'I am happy to hear you speak. I will arrange a phone for you,' the nurse assured the wounded officer with a smile. 'You've been on glucose drips ever since you were brought here unconscious. The upper part of your uniform was soaked in blood, and the lower part was covered in mud and ash. A strong smell of explosives filled the entire room when they brought you here,' she added.

Capt. Akhilesh listened to her quietly. He could relate to every word the nurse had said to him. The blast, the flowing blood, the ice turning black, shelling from the sky and dead bodies everywhere on the ground. The scenes were now frozen in his memory, perhaps for the rest of his life.

'Was I brought here alone, or were there other officers with me?' he asked in the hope of seeing familiar faces around.

'Some soldiers were brought here with you and the bodies of the martyrs have been sent to their homes,' the nurse replied in a low tone.

'Your team established a hold on the Three Pimples area. Our national flag is flying at the top. The entire country is celebrating, but some families will never see their loved ones ever again.' There were tears in her eyes as she continued, 'Some of your brothers from the war were brought here in plywood coffins, including Maj. Acharya, Capt. Vijayant and Capt. Kengurüse of 2 Rajputana Rifles.'

Broken by the news, Capt. Akhilesh cried thinking about the tragic loss of his war brothers. There was nothing one could do but say a silent prayer for the peace of the departed souls and the welfare of their families.

Being based in Srinagar, Mrs Manisha Sharma, wife of Maj. Sharma, and Mrs Goswami visited Capt. Akhilesh as soon as she got the news of his arrival to the hospital. Their presence was like family to Capt. Akhilesh.

In the evening, the nurse arranged a telephone for him. He dialled a number and seconds later, the phone rang in the director's office at Arena Multimedia in Dehradun. My brother, Vishal, who was in the reception area outside, ran in to answer the phone. He instantly recognized the voice.

'How are you, Captain? There's been no news from you recently and we're all worried. Shikha has not eaten for four days now. I am so relieved to hear your voice,' he said, all in one breath.

'Where is she?' asked Akhilesh.

'She is at home. She stopped coming to the institute a few days ago. She just keeps praying to God. Hardly eats, hardly smiles or talks to anyone. How are you?' Vishal repeated his question.

'I am okay, I'm coming to Delhi. I want to speak to Shikha,' Akhilesh said.

'You can call on our landlord's landline number. She will answer. Our landlord moved their phone to our house so she can receive your calls immediately. She's always next to the phone waiting for your call.' Vishal hung up and left for home, where I sat quietly, waiting.

The long ring indicated it was an STD call. I immediately picked up the receiver and could hear him breathing on the other side even before he spoke.

'How are you?' I asked, taking a pause. I just wanted to hear the sound of his voice.

'They are sending me to Delhi. I will reach tomorrow. I'm not sure at what time though,' Akhilesh told me.

Tears rolled down my cheeks as I heard him speak. 'What's happened? You do not sound well. Are you okay?' I inquired. Just hearing his voice and knowing he was alive brought immense relief.

'I hurt my hand. They say I've done my bit, so I can go home.' He continued hiding the truth about the severity of his injuries.

'They're sending you back in the middle of the war, because you hurt your hand?' I asked, unable to hide my disbelief.

He paused, and then asked, 'Aren't you happy?'

'Of course, I am. Your voice has infused new life into me. I've been waiting to see you for months. I just want to tell you that you don't have to hide anything from me. You are back. That is enough for me.' I explained.

He just asked, 'When can I see you?'

'I will be there before you reach. Just tell me where... '

'Base Hospital, Delhi Cantonment.'

While making a note of the location, many questions arose in my mind, but I just said, 'See you tomorrow. Just take care until I get there,' I said, trying to mask my fears.

'I love you. You are the reason I was able to return,' Akhilesh softly said.

'Love you too. I trusted that God would not take you away from me.' I was losing control over the tears that I'd been holding back for months. I placed the receiver down slowly.

My family was sitting next to me, listening to the conversation. They smiled and hugged me. I was still crying. It was the first time I had cried in front of everyone; often, I would cry alone in the middle of the night.

'Pack your things. We will leave for Delhi early tomorrow morning,' Papa told me.

At night, I visited Sai temple to thank God. It was the longest night of my life. I tried to sleep, but the volume of the ticking clock seemed to grow louder with each passing moment. I could count every second. We left for Delhi at 4 a.m. in our green Ambassador. My brother was driving and Papa was seated next to him. Ma and I were in the back seat. Soon, our car was whizzing on the curves of the Mohand hills. No one was in the mood to talk. I don't remember when I fell asleep, but I woke up as we were about to reach Meerut. It took around six hours from Dehradun to Delhi, and then another hour to reach Base Hospital, Delhi Cantt.

Being the daughter of a doctor couple, I had lived in hospital campuses throughout my childhood, but I had never seen anything as huge as the army base hospital in Delhi Cantt. It had wide roads with tall trees at the sides, and it seemed as though scattered old buildings were hidden amid the beautiful green surroundings. We stopped at the reception to the left of the entrance gate. They directed us towards the orthopaedic ward. After crossing a few roads, we reached the orthopaedic officers' ward. There were rooms on both sides of the road. White walls with slanted white roofs, a common corridor and parallel gardens ran along both sides of the road. Small pathways were created to approach the different rooms of the wards. Ortho Officers' Ward 1 was on the right, and Ward 2 was on the left. Each ward contained around 10 rooms, and each room accommodated three beds. There was a staff room at the corner of Ward 1. We inquired about Capt. Akhilesh. The nurse waiting with a list informed us they had not yet arrived. They weren't sure when the wounded soldiers would arrive by the Indian Airlines plane, shuttling between Srinagar and Delhi. I requested Papa to accompany me to buy a bouquet of flowers in the meantime. As Ma settled on the benches in the common corridor, Papa and I went outside the hospital in search of a flower shop, leaving Vishal near the nursing staff room for updates. But we found no shops near the hospital. Google Maps didn't exist back then, you could only rely on memory or ask someone. We were new to the place, and there was no one on the road that we could ask. Unaware that Gopinath and Sadar Bazar that were nearby, we took the inner ring road. After travelling 10 km, I noticed flower shops on the side of the road; it was the entrance to Sarojini Nagar. We returned to the hospital with a beautiful bouquet. Vishal bought us a few patties for lunch from the shop inside the complex, while we waited. Now, everyone was desperate to see Capt. Akhilesh.

After waiting for around three hours, an ambulance arrived and a wheelchair exited the customized ramp. A very skinny, dark person was sitting in the wheelchair. His uniform looked like it was on a clothes hanger instead of his body, and his face was not fully visible because of his cap. His left hand was covered in plaster and fat bandages. A sling was around his neck to support his hand. As he was brought closer, his eyes met my sight. He was the one I had been waiting for, all these months. He looked malnourished and haggard: like a skeleton covered with black skin. They had been fighting a war without proper food; surviving for days without meals. The cold, harsh weather had turned his skin rough and dark. I could not help myself and burst out crying at his condition. But he was smiling without a tear in his eyes. I wanted to hug him and cry louder, but the discipline and traditions of the army held me back. Papa handed the bouquet to Akhilesh as I had completely forgotten about the flowers.

'Welcome back. We are delighted to see you. We are proud of you,' Vishal said while shaking hands with Akhilesh. Then he held me and said, 'Stop crying, look at your husband. He is so brave, still in uniform.'

Akhilesh raised his hand towards me, so I went a little closer and sat on the floor to hold his hand. I tried smiling, but the tears of joy kept falling because I could finally see him alive before my eyes. He held my hand and said, 'I am back for you and because of you. I am happy that I fulfilled my dream, for which I wore the uniform. I am sure it was your love that saved me. It was lady luck who brought me back.' I was just looking deep into his eyes silently; smiling and crying at the same time. We were distracted when the nurse approached us.

'I have to take him for surgery. You can meet him later,' she said politely.

I smiled and gave her way. We kept standing there until she had taken him out of our sight. Lying on the operation table, Akhilesh felt the pinprick of a needle followed by numbness, when the anaesthesia was injected. Drifting in and out of consciousness, he vaguely remembers being placed on a gurney and lying there while the doctor was called. Dr Colonel J. Sikdar, a senior orthopaedic surgeon, operated on Akhilesh with his team. It was intricate repair work that took several hours.

Meanwhile, Papa and my brother went out to look for a place for us to stay but could not find any. Then Papa, being a doctor himself, met the Base Hospital Commandant, Brigadier B.K. Mohanti, who was a very generous gentleman. He immediately ordered his staff to make arrangements for the families of the war heroes to stay on campus. They converted the old barracks into guest rooms. They were situated deep inside the campus, near a huge ground with a helipad in the centre. Vishal and I sat on the bench in the corridor while Papa took Ma to the guest room. That entire day, I thanked God for bringing Akhilesh back alive, even if severely wounded. The bright blue colour of the day turned into purple. The ambulance returned in the evening after a five-hour wait. This time, Akhilesh was unconscious and on a stretcher. The nurse and ward boys immediately took him into room no. 5, and placed him on the bed near the washroom door. There was another patient in the room, on the bed next to the door. He was Captain Lakshya Reddy, who had a fracture on his left hand. He greeted us with a smile. The room was big enough to accommodate three beds, and each bed had one side table and one chair for the attendant. It was neat and clean with all the basic amenities for patients. The nurse asked us to have dinner in the officers' dining hall. I ate a little and then sat down on a chair next to Akhilesh's bed. He was still asleep. Around 9 p.m., the nurse asked us to leave as visiting hours were over by then. I sat on the stairs outside the room, when the nurse asked me to leave from there too.

'Sister, please, I don't want to go. I will just keep sitting here and I won't disturb you or Capt. Akhilesh,' I pleaded.

'How long will you sit?' she asked, concerned.

'All night. He might gain consciousness in some time. I want to be here if he requires anything,' I replied.

'He will not gain consciousness for another five hours. Dr Col Sikdar operated on him and transplanted an iron rod inside his hand to support the broken bone. It was a major operation. The anaesthesia will take a while to wear off,' she explained, before adding, 'I suggest you leave and get some rest. You've been here since morning.'

'I will not be able to sleep. I just want to be by his side when he wakes up. Please let me stay here. I won't disturb anyone,' I pleaded once more.

'But this is an officer's ward, so you can't stay here. There are other patients in the room too.'

'I will sit in the corridor outside the room,' I joined my hands together in request.

She smiled at me and went inside her duty room. It appeared she was busy but understood my feelings. Until morning, my brother and I remain seated on the stairs in front of Akhilesh's room. Sometimes, we would peep from the window. The light in the room was switched off, but the light from the corridor was enough to see. Each time, we found Akhilesh sleeping. Throughout the night, I saw the nurse shuttling from one room to another. She was awake the entire night, and so was I.

I hadn't had a night of sound sleep in months; all those nights without him when he was on the rough terrain of the Kargil peaks. But that day, I was calm and peaceful. It felt like God had blessed two lives by saving one. I promised myself I would continue with the Thursday fasts as an act of thanksgiving for the rest of my life.

SCARS, WOUNDS AND A DISABLED OFFICER

I can only provide medical treatment, but his wellness is in your hands. Just take care of him.

The chirping of birds and the beautiful dawn brought hope the next morning. I saw Akhilesh again when the nurse went into the room to change his drip. His eyes were still shut. She smiled at me and asked, 'Just married?' I nodded in affirmation.

'He will wake up in a couple of hours. You can freshen up in the meantime,' she suggested.

I too wanted to look good when he opened his eyes, so I walked down towards the guest house, feeling content and at peace. We returned to Ortho Ward 1 around 8 a.m. The team of doctors was on its rounds, so we waited outside. My father was also an orthopaedic surgeon, so he and Dr Col Sikdar clicked instantly. The doctor made us aware of the severity of my husband's wounds and the disability he would have to live with.

'He has lost his left palm. I have put in an iron rod for support. The nerves have also broken, so it will take months to bring back functionality to his hand. We will try our best, but his left hand will remain weak. He will require assistance with his day-to-day routine. Moreover, he is traumatized. He has such horrible memories of the brutal war that it will take a decade to overcome them. It is good that your daughter is with him. He is lucky to have her. And she is lucky that he is back.' Dr Col Sikdar explained the case details to Papa while I stood at the side.

Then he turned to me. 'I can only provide medical treatment, but his wellness is in your hands. Just take care of him.' His words were like guidelines for me. I just smiled in response.

While Papa and the doctor were still talking, sharing their army service and government service experiences, I went inside the room. Akhilesh was sitting up in bed. His chapped lips broke into a smile, and his eyes were warm with affection. Ma sat on the chair by his bed while I kept standing. Capt. Reddy brought me a chair, lifting it with one hand.

'Please, don't lift the chair. I will do it myself.' I was embarrassed.

'Ma'am, I have broken my hand, but I'm still an army officer. I can't sit while you are standing,' replied Capt. Reddy.

'He will not be able to have breakfast today. You should eat in the dining hall as breakfast will not be served after 9 a.m.,' the nurse announced as she entered the room.

Akhilesh was weak and on a liquid diet. I helped him sip some tea while the others went for breakfast.

'Inform my parents that I'm here at Base Hospital, Delhi Cantt,' Akhilesh said in a low tone.

'You haven't told them yet?' I asked in surprise.

'I wanted to be fully conscious when they met me. Otherwise, my condition would have upset them deeply,' he said.

'Yes, you're right. I will inform them today,' I assured him.

He slept most of the afternoon as I sat by his side. The nurse came in a few times to change the drip. I went out in search of an STD booth and found one near the entrance gate of the campus. While searching for the phone booth, I met Major Rathore, who was admitted in the room next to Akhilesh's in the same ward, and his wife. Most of the officers were in casual clothes except for Akhilesh, who was in uniform. He wore it so I wouldn't be shocked to see him in that condition, but his weakness revealed everything at first glance. In the evening, I was sitting on the stairs adjacent to the garden. An ambulance arrived again, and a ward boy brought out one more wounded officer on a wheelchair and took him inside the room of Maj. Rathore. He was Dr Capt. Somnath Basu, who had received a shrapnel wound on his left foot. I found out later that he was the same doctor who had administered first-aid to Akhilesh when he came down from the peak.

There was one TV in the room shared by the three patients, but there was no conflict as everyone wanted to watch the same thing – news channels. One could hear the sounds of news bulletin across the corridor from every room. The video telecasts of the funerals of our officers and soldiers. Live reports from the peaks of Kargil. The war was still on. The nation mourned the deaths of its most loyal and sincere sons. Victory seemed to pale in comparison to the sacrifices that soldiers and their families made to achieve it. Everyone was carrying tears and sadness in their eyes.

Dinner was ready to be served in the dining hall, but no one showed up to eat it.

Slowly, Akhilesh's face reflected the agony he was feeling inside. I was observing him while we watched TV. The agony of the death of his war buddies aggravated his pain. He squished his eyes and cried, and his face began to turn purple. I called the nurse immediately.

'Sister, I'm experiencing unbearable pain, as though someone has cut my hand,' he told the nurse. His voice was throbbing with pain and his eyes were moist with tears, as he held his left hand with his right. I supported his right hand as I was scared to touch the injured left hand covered with bandages. Looking at his condition, my eyes turned moist too. Capt. Reddy too came close and sat by the side.

'If both of you cry, then who will console him?' the nurse said with a firm voice. 'The splinters hit you. The pain is obvious. Now be as brave as you were in Kargil, while coming down to the first-aid station after being injured,' the nurse said while injecting Akhilesh with a painkiller.

'I see! When you're alone, you can bear the pain, but if you have someone taking care of you, you let go of yourself. Ma'am is here, so you're trying to get her sympathy,' Capt. Reddy joked in an attempt to ease the situation. He then smiled, and his smile was truly infectious as it made Akhilesh smile too despite the tears in his eyes.

Capt. Reddy's trick seemed to work as Akhilesh seemed to feel slightly more at ease. 'I'm not exaggerating. I am actually suffering. She is my wife. I don't have to earn her sympathy,' he said lightly.

All four of us were smiling now, but the pain was still there. The casual conversation had lightened the mood, but it didn't decrease the pain. Still, it moved our focus away from the tragedy and helped us forget for a while. The nurse permitted me to stay beyond visiting hours. I guess she understood it was the need of the hour. Her patient needed love and attention more than medicine at this point.

I sat on a chair by his bed. The lights in the room were switched off, but the light from the corridor outside provided some visibility. Around midnight, I noticed Akhilesh's restlessness as he tried to mask his pain.

'What's wrong?' I asked as I held his hand.

'The snow had turned black because of continuous artillery shelling. There wasn't even water to drink. We dug deep, looking for clean ice, and sucked on it to quench our thirst. When I close my eyes now, I still see the pools of blood and body parts of my soldier brothers spread all over the snow. It's so tough to advance and continue fighting when the person next to you drops down dead. You don't even have the time to shed a tear over his death, or fear for your own.' He broke down as he told me this; with tears streaming down his face. I was at a loss for words, so I just held his hand to console him, unable to stop my tears. I could visualize the conditions he had experienced at the war front.

Since Capt. Reddy was sleeping on the next bed, I whispered, 'It's important that you sleep to regain your strength.'

'Whenever I close my eyes, I see flashbacks of the war,' Akhilesh told me.

I felt helpless as there wasn't much I could to do comfort him. While it was important to listen to him, it was also crucial for him to sleep. I called the nurse and told her about his torment. After a while, she returned with a syringe in her hand.

'This will help,' she said while injecting the painkiller.

In an hour, Akhilesh was fast asleep. When the nurse came to change his drip, I was still sitting silently on the chair by the side of the bed. She observed the tiredness in my eyes.

'You should get some sleep. It's important that you take care of yourself too. I can see you're not keeping well,' she told me. She was right, I had been through months of sleepless nights, and yet, sleep was the last thing on my mind. But eventually, my eyes grew heavy, so I went to the guest room to rest.

A couple of hours of sleep were sufficient for me, as Akhilesh was constantly on my mind. I took out a set of clothes to dress Akhilesh in after bathing him. Worried about the restrictions of his movements due to the plaster on his hand, I removed the left sleeves of some of his shirts so that he could wear them easily. I got ready and left for the ward while my parents and brother were still sleeping.

When Akhilesh woke up, he asked me to take him for a bath. At the war front, he and many others were deprived of such basic amenities. As I locked the bathroom door from inside, Akhilesh wrapped me with one arm and kissed me passionately on my lips. Then he looked into my eyes and whispered, 'I love you'. I buried my face in his chest and sobbed uncontrollably, saying, 'I've missed you so much'. We remained in that tight embrace. We were alone together after such a long and painful separation. There was so much to say but we could not speak, so we conveyed our feelings through touch. Love doesn't need to be expressed in exotic locations or through expensive gifts. All you need are stolen, private moments away from the world.

I gave him a shave, and then tied his plastered hand to the shower pipe to avoid getting it wet while bathing him. The touch of the free-flowing water on his body brought immense pleasure to his face. I smiled when he took a deep breath to sniff the fragrance of the shampoo. He seemed like he was being treated with luxury.

'It's been months since I've had a proper bath. I am feeling so fresh... ' he said, his voiced filled with content, and then added, 'and loved'. I was smiling, blushing and crying all at once.

After helping Akhilesh have his breakfast, I took all his dirty clothes from Kargil to wash them at the guest room. My family stayed by his side. Two hours later when I returned, I saw my parents sitting on a bench in the corridor outside the room.

'Your in-laws have arrived. We are sitting here because there were too many people in the room. It would disturb other patients,' Papa said calmly, while Ma appeared disturbed. I covered my head with my dupatta and entered the room. I saw Mummyji sitting beside Akhilesh and weeping. Her close friend was standing by her side consoling her. As I approached to touch Mummyji's feet, her friend raised her hand to stop me and yelled at me in front of everyone present in the room.

'You go away. You are the reason for her son's suffering. He was fine until you came into his life. You have no respect for customs and tradition. Your ignorance sent her son to war. You will never, ever wear that lehenga again. How are you people not aware of such customs? Our son has paid for your mistakes. Once, I even saw you without toe rings. You don't understand the value of bindi, bangles, sindoor and toe rings. A married woman needs to wear all of this.' My parents too heard the harsh words in her high-pitched voice, while they were seated outside.

I was stunned; I stood there trembling in disbelief at what she had just said to me. My mother-in-law kept her head down, weeping – she didn't even look at me. I realized the dominance of her friend over her. My throat felt heavy and I lost my voice. I finally realized why Mummyji never spoke to me whenever I called them at Moradabad. She despised me and believed I was unlucky for her son. This thought left me deeply hurt and shattered. Even now, I remember the agony I experienced in those moments. I just looked around at everyone; they seemed shocked and were quiet too. I was shattered at being tagged unlucky for the person I loved the most. I kept standing there and sobbing while she unleashed her anger on me for a few more minutes, while nobody stopped her. Each hate-filled word stabbed me like a weapon. I left the room crying, and ran straight to the guest room and shut the door. My parents wished to avoid any further scenes in the ward so they left without speaking to anyone, and returned to the guest room. After they had knocked on the door a few times, I opened the door and hugged Ma with my tears still flowing. She just consoled me without a word, by gently patting my head.

After a while, Papa said, 'Don't worry, beta. Your mother-in-law is upset. Don't take those words to heart. It's shocking for her to see her son in this state. She is disturbed that's why she didn't stop her friend. Everything will be okay in a few days.'

My heart was not willing to accept that I was unlucky for the one I loved the most. 'Papa, do you also think I am the reason for all this suffering?' I asked in a broken voice.

'Beta, you are the reason for his return from the war zone. That was a miracle. No soldier wishes for war, but he prepares for it all the time. Risking one's life to fight the enemy is part of his profession. And he's done his duty well,' Ma said. 'It's human nature to blame someone for painful circumstances. They want to relate it to somebody's mistakes. It's not right, but all we can do is wait until this difficult phase passes,' she continued. 'It's not just her thoughts that she is expressing. These are the beliefs of the society she lives in. '

'This lady is not a stranger. She is the mother of the one you love the most, so for the sake of your husband, forgive her. She is traumatized now, so just let it go. She will realize her mistake later.'

'What should I do?' I asked Ma, while weeping in her lap.

'Just listen to your heart. If you believe you are lucky for your husband, no customs or traditions can affect you. Just love and support him unconditionally. Have faith in your love and in God. Nothing can go wrong.' Ma's eyes were calm and peaceful as she spoke to me. Her guidance was like a silver ray of hope bursting through the dark clouds in my life. As I looked at her, she appeared like a goddess to me.

My family travelled back to Dehradun as the hospital had only four guest rooms, all occupied by relatives of other patients, and Papaji, Mummyji and her friend needed a place to rest too. I stayed back to be with Akhilesh, so we didn't have to share the guest room under those harrowing circumstances. I avoided being alone with them. When they were in the ward, I kept away, and when they returned to the guest room, I left for the ward. I sat by Akhilesh's side the entire night, without a word. Even the nurse didn't order me to leave after visiting hours. Akhilesh could see how hurt and upset I was. He felt awful about his mother's behaviour, but remained quiet. We both didn't wish to hurt anyone.

The next morning, my in-laws returned to Moradabad and their respective workplaces. As they were leaving, I touched their feet again and, in return, Mummyji said sorry to me in a low voice. But the damage was beyond repair. I could not forget those moments. Today, 23 years after the incident, its memory still fills my eyes with tears.

At the time, my wounded husband required my love and support, so I locked my agony inside a box and set it aside. However, it was also important to me to regain my mental strength, peace and self-confidence. I decided to stand up for myself; not to disregard anyone but to build my self-esteem. I'd brought good fortune to my husband; I was sure of it. For a soldier, it's an honour to fight for his country, and Capt. Akhilesh had that honour. He had been passionate about being an army officer since childhood. It was a dream come true for him, and not a misfortune at all. And it was my destiny to share my life with him. This thinking and firm belief made our relationship stronger than ever. We were able to defeat society's ruthless criticism, which only creates rifts between family members. From that day onwards, I stopped believing in any symbols of marriage. My only faith was my belief in myself, my unconditional love for my husband, and my devotion to God. Everything else is just superficial. No bindi, bangles, sindoor, or toe rings can protect my love, only I can do that. No harm can come to Akhilesh as long as we were protected by the Almighty. And I am the daughter of God. He will never leave my side.

DEFEATING MISFORTUNE

It's a story of pain with pride; one that will make you teary with grief yet bring a smile to your face. A story where death is not THE END.

I witnessed a daily sight as I walked from the guest room to the officers' ward in the mornings. Near a crossroad, the hospital staff would be carrying coffins towards the mortuary. These were the bodies of our brave soldiers who had made the ultimate sacrifice in the Kargil War. I would join my hands together in prayer for the departed and their family members, who would receive their coffins with broken hearts. *How would they handle receiving them when my eyes well up just looking at the coffins?* I prayed to God to give them the courage to face the bitter truth of an ugly war, as ultimately, they were the sufferers. For them, time had stood still, and they would never see their loved ones again. The country was losing its most sincere, loyal and brave sons. People would always remember them with honour, but this could never make up for the void felt by their loved ones.

The coffins were not the only observations I made on a daily basis. In the evenings, I would visit the small food joint on campus and I would see many soldiers. Some on their feet, some on wheelchairs, and some on stretchers across the road. This food stall was near the soldier's ward;

I could see ambulances pulling up to drop them off, and the hospital staff helping them into the ward. They were all wounded soldiers; each one had a part or parts of their body missing. Some would never walk again, some would never see again, and some had lost their limbs. Some of them had their bones crushed into such tiny pieces that doctors had to piece them together with steel rods and screws. The wounds on their bodies were covered in bandages, while their sombre faces and vacant eyes bore testimony to the torment they had endured. They would struggle with the smallest tasks for the rest of their lives. Their disabled status would get them downgraded in the army on medical grounds. The army would not ask them to leave, but their self-respect would not let them stay.

Each and every victory on the peaks of the Kargil was achieved by paying a heavy price. The evening news always brought gloom to the ward. Happiness about victories would soon fizzle out with the news of the injuries and deaths of soldiers. More than the physical wounds, the strain of the war zone was causing discomfort. Each day's tragic news made it even more difficult for the injured officers to overcome their pain. Often, Akhilesh would wake up from convulsions in his dreams in the middle of the night. He was haunted by the harrowing images of war: blood on the ground, snow turned black, smoke everywhere, the bloody wounds of his comrades and him directing artillery fire. He would scream and say he wanted to go back and fight the enemy. The pain in his wounded hand would shoot up suddenly, and the rest of the night would be spent suffering. The nurse usually injected him with a painkiller to decrease the pain and help him sleep. Now, she wanted me to stay back at night as well, so someone was always by his side. The situation was getting worse. The need of the hour was to help these officers recuperate. A stress-free environment was essential to their recovery.

Once Akhilesh was able to move around in a wheelchair, he asked me to take him to the soldiers' ward. He wanted to meet his men as he could relate to their mental condition and suffering.

It was a huge dormitory with beds lined up on both sides, leaving space to walk in between. There were around 15 beds in one room, and at the end of the room was a door leading to the next room. There were television sets on the walls between every four beds. A hospital staff counter was inside the ward, and nurses were always around. On seeing Capt. Akhilesh and me, the soldiers in the ward became emotional and had tears in their eyes.

'*Sahab, ab main kya karunga?* (Sir, what will I do now?)' Rifleman Madhav Singh was sobbing. Both his legs had been amputated. '*Ab main apne paon pe kabhi khada nahi ho sakta.* (Now, I can never stand on my legs).' He was extremely depressed. '*Mere chhote bacche hain, biwi hai, budhe ma-baap hain. Ab un sab ki dekhbhal kaun karega?* (I have young kids, a wife and old parents. Who will provide for them now?)' Capt. Akhilesh extended his hand to console him, and Rifleman Singh started howling. '*Main marna chahta hun, sahab. Ek apaang ki zindagi nahin ji sakta.* (Sir, I want to die. I can't live life as a disabled person).' His sobs echoed through the entire ward. It was gut-wrenching to watch him in so much pain.

'*Tu sipahi ho kar rota hai? Tune desh ke liye apne paon gavaye hai. Fauj tera khayal rakhegi* (You are a soldier, and you are crying? You have lost your legs while fighting for your country. The army will take care of you and your family),' Capt. Akhilesh assured him.

'Sahab, fauj toh khayal rakhegi magar jeena to hume hi hai. Bina haathon ke main apne parivar walon pe hamesha hi nirbhar rahunga. Isse accha to mai yuddh mein mar jaata. (Sir, we know the army will take care of us, but we are the ones who will go through life with our disabilities. Without my hands, I will always be dependent on my family. It would have been better if I had died at the war front).' It was the voice of Sepoy Vishnu Sharma from the next bed.

'Sahab, yeh sach ab kabhi nahi badlega. Meri aankhon ke aage sirf andhera hai (Sir, the bitter truth of life will not change for me. There is only darkness before my eyes),' said Rifleman Jaswant Singh from the next bed.

There were so many questions, so much uncertainty and so much sorrow that the atmosphere turned heavy and gloomy. Even the nurses present had moist eyes. Everyone was looking at us as though we could explain the miserable conditions life had imposed on them.

Then Capt. Akhilesh asked them this question, *'Kya tumhe ladai mein jaane ka afsos hai?* (Do you all regret fighting the war against the enemy to protect out county)?'

'Nahi, Sahab. Mauka mile to hum fir jaenge. Apne desh ke liye hum jaan bhi de sakte hain. (No, sir, we will go again if given a chance. We are willing to sacrifice our lives for our country),' Havaldar Gurudev Singh said, and the others nodded in agreement.

'Hume ladai mein jaane ka nahin, apaang ho jaane ka dukh hai. (We do not regret fighting for our country. We just regret coming back disabled),' Havaldar Singh explained.

'Martyrdom is an honour achieved only by the luckiest. The rest will have to find glory in their disabilities. You are all soldiers who fought for your country. No one can ever take away this pride from you. You have done the greatest service to the nation,' Capt. Akhilesh reminded them.

One soldier was covered with bandages from head to toe, and had one of his hands amputated. He was quiet, and his wife was sitting next to him. I inquired about his injuries. She told me a grenade went off just as he entered an enemy bunker. Splinters had penetrated his entire body, making cuts on his skin. There was nothing left anymore: his eyes, face, hands, legs or stomach. He was alive because he was still breathing. I then asked her, 'After the bandages are removed, he may appear unattractive. He may never be able to use his hands or see or walk. Are you happy he is back?'

She started crying. '*Memsaab, yeh zinda hai mere liye yahi bahut hai. Mere bacche use dekhkar bade ho jayenge* (He is breathing and alive. That is sufficient for me. At least my kids will grow up around him).'

I turned to Rifleman Singh and said, 'It's easy for a person to die but difficult for family members to accept his death. Now, for the sake of your family, learn to live with a smile. You will figure out how to handle the rest over time.' He nodded in acknowledgement.

While returning, Akhilesh and I continued thinking about the conversations in the soldiers' ward. We stopped at the eating joint, had small cups of tomato soup, and quietly watched a few kids playing in the adjacent garden. Life must go on no matter what; it is important to be happy with whatever you have in hand. We began visiting the soldiers' ward often, as we felt it was our responsibility to take care of our soldiers and their families. In the army, the officers and their wives always prioritize the welfare of their soldiers and their families.

Soon, the middle bed of our room was occupied by Captain Naveen Anaberu Nagappa. He arrived with steel rods and screws in both legs and grief in his heart. He was a young, south Indian gentleman with a permanently sad expression on his face who barely spoke or smiled. He was from 13 JAK Rifles and was with Capt. Vikram Batra during the attack of Point 4875. They pulled him back when he was severely injured during the attack, but Capt. Batra made the supreme sacrifice and died a martyr. Two weeks later, Captain Satendra Sangwan from 16 Grenadiers was moved into a room nearby, after being injured during an operation in Kargil.

In an effort to distract the officers from the stress of the war, we bought playing cards and began playing rummy. Soon, officers from the other rooms joined us too and we formed a group. We gradually became friends.

The Chief of Army Staff, and his wife, president of AWWA, visited us one morning. Their presence immediately uplifted the mood of the officers. I noticed a remarkable difference in the energy levels of the officers, who had been up since morning to meet their chief. It was nice to see dutiful, sincere and loyal officers around. That day, they had taken a temporary break from their pain and discomfort. It was my first meeting with General V.P. Malik and Mrs Ranjana

Malik; they were genuinely concerned about us all. I was struck by their aura while they were talking to Akhilesh and me. The general warmly patted his captain on the back and asked me to write about my experiences of the army and war as a newly-wed. He said, 'Years later, you will look back and reflect on these memories, and there will be a sense of achievement in your heart.' Today, I can relate to how true his words were.

The news about the wretched environment in the soldiers' and the officers' wards must have reached the commander of the Base Hospital. He opened the hospital gates, from 11 a.m. to 1 p.m., for people who wished to meet the Kargil War heroes, to thank and honour them for their bravery and sacrifices.

One morning while feeding Akhilesh his breakfast, through the window, I saw many school children lined up in the corridor outside. The nurse came inside and informed us that the kids wished to meet their war heroes. They were carrying cards, chocolates and letters for the wounded officers. A sense of pride overwhelmed Akhilesh and his eyes welled up. That morning, I learned a significant lesson: Stay focused on the positive elements of life. When there is darkness all around, and you want to come out of the tunnel that sucks you in, focus on the ray of light at the end of the tunnel and keep walking towards it.

Visitors waiting to meet the Kargil War heroes and their families soon became a regular feature of the morning. It's always nice to know you are appreciated for your contribution, admired as a hero and acknowledged for your sacrifices. This daily interaction with the citizens of our country infused new energy into everyone around. We were no longer strangers to these people, and they always met us with affection and respect. Laughter returned to the group, and the officers regained their lost smiles. Even the media began interacting with us for stories about the real situation at Kargil and soldiers fighting at the warfront.

A specific group of women too began visiting us daily. Some would bring fresh flowers and arrange them in the vases, and some were experts in Reiki; a way of channelling the energy of the cosmos to heal the body and mind. I noticed Akhilesh sleeping calmly after receiving healing energy from these masters in Reiki. To me, it was an unusual but effective way to provide relief to someone in pain. I requested these ladies to teach me Reiki. With the commandant's permission, they organized a workshop at the officers' ward, and I got the opportunity to be introduced to this amazing healing practice. I found it so effective that I did my foundation course and then my master's in Reiki. Soon, Akhilesh no longer required injections to ease his pain and sleep at night, and I began providing Reiki to most of the wounded officers and soldiers. Meditation had an incredible effect on my inner self as well, and I grew into a positively radiant person who was strong from the inside.

It was the morning that established glory in the history of modern India. All the newspapers were flooded with the headlines: India declared 26 July 1999 as 'Kargil Vijay Diwas' (Kargil Victory Day). The Indian Army had declared a successful culmination of 'Operation Vijay', declaring victory after an almost three-month-long battle on the frosty peaks of Kargil. Drass had been cleared of all intruders. We all shed tears of joy. It was a day for rejoicing and the officers decided to celebrate it with their soldiers. They all chipped in and ordered exotic dishes from restaurants and, with the help of the hospital staff, had the soldiers' ward decorated with flowers, lights and balloons. We invited the staff to join in too, and they accepted the treat with pleasure.

'*Sahab, aaj hume koi shikayat nahin hai. Hamara apang hona sarthak ho gaya* (Sir, we don't have any complaints today. Our disability has a significant victory).' War-wounded soldiers said with proud smiles on their faces.

They danced with their crutches, glucose bottles held up in the air, on one leg, without any hands. Some were on wheelchairs, and some were bandaged from head to toe. I placed myself in one corner, helping them have their meals. It was immensely satisfying to watch them all. I was also relieved knowing that the war had ended and no more coffins would be unloaded from the ambulances in the mornings, and no more disabled soldiers would arrive from Kargil in shock and grief.

One morning, I was sitting beside Akhilesh as he slept. Someone opened the door, and two familiar faces entered the room. My eyes widened in surprise, looking at them as they signalled me not to disturb the sleeping officer. They pulled up a couple of chairs and sat on the other side of the bed. They were well-known celebrities, actors Anupam Kher and Pooja Batra, who had flown from Mumbai to Delhi to meet and honour these real-life heroes. They waited patiently until Akhilesh opened his eyes. They had come to invite us as chief guests on 'Aye Watan Tere Liye', the show they all were organizing at Nehru Stadium in honour of the Kargil warriors.

It was like a dream we had never imagined. We were made to sit in the chief guests' seats, surrounded by film stars. We had permanent smiles on our faces. I spotted Amitabh Bachchan and expressed to a volunteer my desire to meet him. After a few seconds, I saw Amitabh Bachchan coming towards us. He joined his palms together and said, 'You are a noble daughter of our country. We are grateful to you and your husband for fighting for India.' His gratitude, humility and grace touched us deeply. We joined our palms together in response, and Akhilesh said, 'We were just doing our duty. Losing one hand for my country is not a big deal. I have more limbs to sacrifice for the pride of my India.'

Aishwarya Rai and her mother came to pay their respects too. Shatrughan Sinha, Salman Khan, Shilpa Shetty, Udit Narayan and his son, Usha Uthup and several others came to meet the war heroes and their families. Anupam Kher hosted the show and the other stars danced and sang, filling the atmosphere with rhythm and melody. Jaya Bachchan introduced her son, Abhishek Bachchan, to the public for the first time, and Rani Mukherji made an appearance too. At the end, they took Capt. Akhilesh and other officers and soldiers to the stage. Capt. Sangwan sang the song '*Aye Mere Watan Ke Logo*' and Capt. Akhilesh gave a speech. 'My dear countrymen, today, looking at everyone here, my heart is filled with immense pride and assurance. We just need your humble support, love and respect. I guarantee we are enough to drag the enemies out of our country. We will never hesitate to sacrifice ourselves in the service of our nation. The only thing we require while fighting is to see you all standing in our support if we look back. I will never regret my wounded hand as I have the hands of 90 million friends. If my friend loses his leg, he has the support of 90 million countrymen. If I do not return from the war front, there will be 90 million sons for my mother's welfare. A soldier willing to die for his country wants nothing else.' The crowd filling the entire Nehru Stadium was now overwhelmed with emotion, and they honoured the nation's heroes with a standing ovation.

Appreciation can create the most positive vibrations. The effect of the applause from their countrymen brought a glow to the faces of the wounded officers and soldiers, and left me feeling overwhelmed with gratitude too. We learned to wear our wounds as our medals. There was no more regret in our hearts. There was now just an ocean of love for our country and the motivation to dedicate every action to it.

Several gatherings were held to honour the families of martyrs and disabled soldiers. The selfless duty and sincerity of soldiers found the endorsement of the people for whom they had sacrificed everything. The wave of patriotism was so strong that every person we met was in tears and could feel the pain of the soldiers and their families during the war.

Capt. Akhilesh was awarded a wound medal by the Indian Army, and a green card by the government of India, recognizing his contribution to the victory at Kargil. This green card offers him priority on his visits to any government officials. The victory of Kargil is not a story of just winning. It's a story of pain with pride; one that will make you feel proud even as your eyes turn moist. A story where death is not 'THE END'. There are many inspiring tales woven into the story of valour and courage displayed by the Kargil soldiers. The most junior officers of the units won the battles, as the plans of senior officers often went up in smoke due to enemy shelling. The youngsters of the unit were the driving forces on the peaks; climbing the mountains, leading from the front and making quick decisions. India had a new set of legends now. These stories attracted Bollywood to the Base Hospital, the most accessible place for them to meet wounded heroes and collect first-hand information about the war. Aamir Raza Husain approached us with his team to get details of the Kargil War, for his stage show *Fifty Day War*, and film maker J.P. Dutta's team came to conduct research for their movie *LOC Kargil*.

Shaheed teri maut hi
Tere watan ki zindagi,
Tere lahun se jaag
Uthegi is chaman ki zindagi,
Khilenge phool uss
Jagah pe tu jahan shaheed ho.

GOODBYE UNIFORM

It's not what you lost that counts; it's what you do with what's left.

Post the war, there was one more battle the wounded soldiers were fighting, and it was to regain their strength physically, mentally and professionally. Day and night, I remained at the hospital by Akhilesh's side to assist him with everything that he needed help with. The wounds on his hand were healing, but the functionality was still missing. After weeks, when the doctor removed the bandages and splint, his wrist went limp and his palm dropped without any feeling. It was one of the most disturbing moments for us. More than the sight of stitches and swelling, it was the lack of sensation and the inability to move his fingers that made us realize how badly he had been injured.

Doctors performed another surgery to reconnect the tendons. They gave him an anaesthesia injection in the neck that blocked all sensations in the body. Again, it was a complex procedure with delicate repair work taking several hours. Both ends of each severed tendon had to be retrieved and stretched to the point where they could be fastened together.

To keep Akhilesh away from sinking into despondency, I started taking him out on long drives. Sometimes, we'd go out on a day pass. And sometimes, we'd sneak out after I stuffed his bed with pillows covered by a blanket, to make it look like he was sleeping. I drove him to most of Delhi's tourist spots during these outings. Life kept giving us disappointments, but we continued celebrating life. It was a blessing that he had come back alive from the war, and no other ugly facts could make us sad again. He'd wear his wounds with pride, just as he wore his medals. All our first festivals after marriage were celebrated at the hospital. My first home was that small guest room at Base Hospital, where I spent nearly one year looking at the moon wax and wane.

A few months later, when the doctor removed the bandages, his hand looked grotesque. Swollen and stiff, it seemed mummified. The dry skin was taut and peeling. I could see the black marks of stitches on his skin and the traces of dried blood that remained beneath his nails. The wounds made it look like someone else's hand had been attached to Akhilesh's wrist – amputated and transplanted from a corpse. It was weak, flaccid and trembling from having been immobilized for almost a year.

Doctors continued his medical treatment and added physiotherapy to the daily process. We were still not disheartened, but it was a long time to be in a hospital so we requested a discharge. The Commandant of the Base Hospital accepted our written application on the grounds that Capt. Akhilesh be posted in Delhi in order to continue the treatment under his supervision.

Before resuming his duty, Akhilesh wished to visit his hometown. The community of Moradabad, where I was once tagged an unlucky bride, now honoured their daughter-in-law with all the compassion they could gather. We stayed there for a month, and each day some organization, corporation or social group hosted a celebration to welcome their brave son and his bride. All the hard feelings of the past vanished with the affection and warmth that people extended to us.

After being discharged from Base Hospital, Akhilesh was posted at Headquarters Delhi Area, and we began our new lives. The permanent disability had limited Capt. Akhilesh to be inside an office, away from the action. He would never be allowed to operate on the frontlines again. He would always be restricted to administrative jobs behind military operations. The person who loved action was slowly getting frustrated with the desk job. His dissatisfaction dragged him down and disheartened him.

'I didn't join the Indian Army to work at a desk. If I must do this for the rest of my life, I would rather accept new challenges outside than remain a liability to the army,' he said one day in frustration, as I drove him home after physiotherapy.

We were allotted temporary accommodation near Taurus Club. It was a single officers' residence, a one-room apartment. Every morning, I assisted him in getting ready, dropped him at his office, and then picked him up in the evening to take him for physiotherapy. Akhilesh had always been a hardworking and intelligent person. He had left Delhi College of Engineering midway to join his dream destination, the NDA. I could tell that he was upset over the restrictions life had imposed on him. He was turning bitter and angry. I was the only person he could express his irritation or grievances to, the only person he asked for support and love, and the only person who witnessed his uneasy sleep.

One Sunday, at the breakfast table, I asked him, 'Are you unhappy?'

'I am trying my best. This useless hand is not working. How long will I have to go for physiotherapy? It's been almost 18 months, and this hand is still hanging in a sling around my neck,' he replied in frustration.

'I know one hand is not functional, but your mind and other hand are working fine,' I said calmly.

'What are you trying to say?' he asked.

'If this disabled hand is making you uncomfortable, shift your focus and forget about it. Work with your mind and use your other hand. You are a bright person, so go back to your studies. I know you can do much better than what you're doing right now. We will make the transition into civilian life. Let's start from scratch. You prepare for the Master of Business Administration (MBA) entrance exams,' I spelled out my intention.

'What are you saying? Leaving the army is like quitting my childhood dreams, my passion and my world. The Indian Army is deep-rooted within me. It will be extremely difficult for me. I have been a soldier since I was in class 6 at the Sainik School. I have given 15 years of my life to this profession.' He was staring at me in disbelief.

'Try and understand. It's important that you are content and happy with your job. You've achieved what you wanted to achieve here. Many army officers don't get to experience real action their entire lives. They keep practising with dummy situations. You had the opportunity to lead your troops in the war zone. You re-established our tricolour on the peaks of Kargil, that was your greatest achievement in the army uniform. Now, there is no higher goal for you here.' I tried to convince him.

He still couldn't digest the notion that leaving the army was an option. He just left without saying a word. A few days later, he went to the South Block Headquarters to seek advice from his seniors. He met the Adjutant General to find a solution to his dilemma.

'Since you have such severe and permanent injuries, it will be very difficult for you to indulge in the physical trainings. It's not only about leaving the army; it's about working to your optimum potential. You are young, brilliant and hardworking. I am sure any civilian organization would be glad to hire you,' the Adjutant General explained.

'Sir, I can't imagine myself without the uniform. I have dedicated my life to the service of my nation,' Capt. Akhilesh replied.

'Who says you can't serve your nation without a uniform? To serve your country in any profession or sector, you need to be just as dedicated as a soldier. And you've been a soldier since childhood. I'm sure you will do well and continue serving the nation no matter where you are,' the Adjutant General said with a gentle smile. 'You're too young to carry the burden of disability in the army for the rest of your life. You will never be questioned for your physical disability outside. But if you stay in the army, you will always be reminded of your physically challenged status on every posting and every operation. You will never achieve SHAPE-1 status for any of the physical activities in the army; and the army, as you know, is all about physical fitness,' he added to explain the situation to his confused junior.

I was waiting in the parking lot when Akhilesh returned with a worried face. I asked nothing and drove us home silently. He was sitting out in the front veranda staring at our flower pots, when I joined him with tea and cheese balls. I was sure he wasn't looking at the plants, but thinking deeply instead.

After a few sips of tea, he told me about the conversation with his senior.

'Why should I start with the entrance exams? I can apply for jobs right away,' he said.

'I know you can get a job easily, but I think our foundation should be strong while we make a transition. You have only developed your defence skills so far, but you will need to acquire business skills for a corporate environment. Don't be in a hurry,' I proposed.

'So, you want me to study? You know, I've never wanted to study after class 12,' he confessed, laughing.

'But in the army too, one has to answer exams that are mandatory for promotions,' he added.

'I will get the prospectuses of the best management colleges in India. You will need to clear the entrance exams first, then its two years of study. Finally, you'll have the most prestigious companies approaching you with job offers,' I assured him.

'I know you're the right person to guide me, as you've undergone the process yourself while preparing for your exams. I've never researched anything other than the army. Thank you so much for being there for me,' Akhilesh said with gratitude.

We discovered his problem was not just a disabled hand, but a lack of zeal. He needed to do something fulfilling. Sometimes, we focus on the immediate hurdles and miss the big picture. And sometimes, it's not about the problem; it's about making the decisions. It wasn't easy for us to decide to leave the army with its secure job and familiar environment. Above all, the army was the only organization Akhilesh had wanted to join since childhood. It was a tough decision for both of us.

A few days later, Capt. Akhilesh received a call from Mr Satish Pradhan, HR Head of the Tata Group. He wished to meet the brave warrior and invited him to the Taj Palace, New Delhi. When Akhilesh entered the lobby, an executive directed him towards Mr Pradhan, waiting at a corner table in the coffee house. The meeting had been scheduled for an hour, but it went on for a few hours as they were engrossed in the conversation. Mr Pradhan offered Akhilesh a job right there, on the spot.

'We will be glad to hire you. You're an intelligent and well-deserving candidate. It is our duty to look after the welfare of war heroes such as you. Never think of yourself as being alone in your struggle. The Tata Group will always support you,' Mr Pradhan said, immediately making a call to his subordinate to draft an offer letter for Akhilesh.

'Sir, are you offering me a job because of my services to the nation on the battlefront? I don't want you to offer me a job because of your sympathy towards my disabilities. I deserve a job based on my abilities. Sorry sir, right now, I can't accept your offer, but I promise I will join Tata Group the day you are able to offer me a job based on my professional competency.'

Mr Pradhan was stunned; this wasn't the answer he had expected. He couldn't believe his ears, but was impressed with Capt. Akhilesh's attitude nevertheless. He saw before him a stubborn, young fighter, and caught a glimpse of a firm leader who will not compromise on his self-respect. It was difficult to believe that a disabled war hero had rejected a job offer from Tata Group, for the sake of his values.

'The offer letter will reach you in a few weeks. Take your time,' the mature business head said calmly, before adding, 'Save my number. You can call me anytime, even if you reject the offer. You've really made an impression on me.'

A few weeks later, as promised, we received the offer letter from Tata Group, but Akhilesh stood firm on his decision.

We were allotted a house at Kirby Place, Delhi Cantt. It was a lovely bungalow surrounded by greenery. There were three rooms in a row, a veranda at the back and a kitchen. We set up the middle room as a study, with a computer table for me and a desk for Akhilesh. He studied while I set up a multimedia company, Excellence Enterprises, so I could work from home at my convenience. I took up project-based work with some companies, creating websites, animations and doing video editing. This was a boon as I was required to be home to assist Akhilesh with his daily routine as well as drive him to the office and hospital. Furthermore, I was carrying my first baby. Yes, I wanted a job, but motherhood was an enormous responsibility and I didn't want to fail at it. I believe that if you don't have the time, you shouldn't bring kids into this world. Due to his office duties during the day, Akhilesh could only find time to study in the evenings. We would work until late at night, hitting the bed at 2 a.m. sometimes. Often, we'd lie awake until the morning discussing the uncertainties we were about to encounter with a baby and living outside the army environment. We were preparing ourselves for the worst circumstances and planning our best solutions. No change is smooth; it's better to be prepared to burn the midnight oil in order to achieve success.

Soon, I was approaching my due date. My blood is 'A negative', a rare blood group that can be complicated for pregnant women. My delivery had to be handled with a lot of precaution to ensure that both my baby and I remained out of danger. Being a gynaecologist surgeon, Ma wanted me to live with her in Dehradun. But I could not leave Akhilesh alone with the struggles of life, even for a day. She travelled every month from Dehradun for my check-up as she was worried about her child, as I was for mine. Once a mother, always a mother.

Akhilesh's mother too stayed with us for a month as I approached the delivery date. There was a day's gap between Mummyji's departure to Moradabad and my mother's arrival. The only day we found ourselves alone with no restrictions, so we attended the wedding reception of Akhilesh's course-mates Captain Samresh Malhotra along with some other friends including Captain Deven Pandey. And that was when my baby decided to come into my arms! We returned from the party and my water bag burst at midnight. I was confused as there were still 18 days to go for the delivery date. We somehow managed to drive to Army Hospital (R&R), and Akhilesh rang up his friends for support. Capt. Pandey came running, completely clueless; until that night he hadn't even noticed my pregnancy! Both friends sat outside the operation theatre, making calls to our parents while I was screaming in pain inside. It was unbearable, and I was wet with perspiration and tears. This continued until 5 a.m., when I finally had a normal delivery. It was 10 April 2001 when a soft, pink, little angel with her tiny head full of curls came into my world. She was exquisite, like a flower or a dewdrop; the most magnificent creature I had ever seen in my entire life. I forgot all my pain and discomfort the moment the doctor handed her to me. The nurse brought me outside the operation theatre, where everyone was waiting for me. We felt blessed and thanked God for this adorable gift. We named our daughter Hirushi – a Sanskrit word that means shining diamond.

Our parents could not stay longer because of their jobs. My baby was most active at night. Even with all the post-delivery pain, I would play with her, sing for her and feed her. I avoided disturbing Akhilesh as he was busy preparing for his MBA entrance exams. I completed my in-hand projects and refused to take on further work. My tired and sleepless eyes were no longer able to take the strain of the computer screen. Even when I was exhausted, I always rustled up the strength to care for my baby doll. Motherhood requires the most responsible and dedicated mode. I was puked upon, peed on and spent sleepless nights cradling my baby, but I wouldn't have had it any other way. My body isn't 'magazine perfect' anymore, but I see a mother when I look in the mirror. And there is no greater honour, love or blessing. I never realized my potential and strength before I became a mother. The amount of stress, pain, and tireless work a mother can manage is beyond imagination for anyone else.

The struggles of life multiplied with the arrival of a baby. We became more dedicated and focused on achieving our goals. When there is no option left, the only way is to face the difficulties and find solutions. The uncertainty of the outside world sometimes puzzled us, and made us question our decision to leave the army. Then again, we concluded that only a satisfied person could create a happy environment. The first step towards getting somewhere is deciding you don't want to stay where you are. All his efforts and hard work paid off and Akhilesh was selected by some of the top management colleges for a full-time MBA course. He chose the Faculty of Management Studies (FMS) as it was in Delhi. In a kind and supportive gesture, the Indian Army allowed us an extension on our accommodation, and Akhilesh could continue his treatment at the Base Hospital alongside his studies.

The army officer who earlier thought of computers as boring now realized their importance. I took charge of all his assignments as he had to submit them in digital form. Akhilesh found it difficult to cope with all the new study methods, along with his job and treatment. With my small baby, I worked regardless of whether it was day or night to support him. On the brighter side, the results of the physiotherapy sessions were now showing and the strength of Akhilesh's hand was improving. He began taking care of his daily routine on his own. Most of the time, he was busy with his studies as his first semester exams were approaching. With no Ola or Uber services available back then days, you had to find your own way. Somehow, Akhilesh managed to start riding a motorbike and travelling on his own.

One afternoon, when he was returning from the exam centre after the first exam, a car took a U-turn without giving any indication. A head-on collision took place with Akhilesh's bike and he was flung six feet away. He suffered a deep impact on the left side of his body. His helmet had fallen off and he hurt his head too. There was a pause in the traffic as everyone was shocked. The car owner was not in a position to escape from the situation. He came out to look for Akhilesh, who was still in shock on the road.

Holding his bleeding hand, the same hand that had been in bandages for a year, he asked the car owner to drop him to the Base Hospital, Delhi Cantt. Leaving the bike there, they rushed to the hospital. When I heard about the accident, I quickly went to the hospital carrying my baby. Akhilesh was admitted to the ICU for observation as the cuts on his left hand and leg were deep, and there were some on his face and one on his head too. It was disheartening to see him injured again. It was also clear from his condition that he wouldn't be able to answer the rest of his exams. It can be tough to keep your calm and be patient in such a situation, especially when you've dedicated all your attention and time towards one goal. Against the doctor's advice, Akhilesh asked me to take him to the exam centre the very next day, directly from the hospital. I got my infant ready with all her paraphernalia and drove Akhilesh to the centre. At the exam centre, everyone was horrified to see a person with bandages all over his body. What they didn't know is that the mental strength of a war hero is more powerful than most people can imagine. I sat in my car all day, while Akhilesh took his exams with bandages around his hand, leg and even face.

God was kind, and we were brave; each time we somehow gathered the courage to overcome the challenges life threw at us. Each hurdle made us stronger. Two years went by amid books, computers and a growing infant. In the same way that carbon turns into diamond under constant pressure, we too created our future. Akhilesh ranked first in his batch and passed out with a gold medal from FMS. He was also selected for the position of Strategic Program Manager at Wipro, through campus interviews. And so, life set us on a new journey into the civilian world. I never wanted a lonely only child and had no doubts about having a second one. By the time we got out of the army environment, I had my son in my arms. We named him Akshat, a combination of both our names. It also means a warrior who will remain intact under any circumstances.

Leaving behind his lifelong dreams of being in the army and settling down in civilian life was not easy for Akhilesh. We had to create a new life from scratch, find our base again and lay a new foundation for an unknown life. At the time, our honourable prime minister, Atal Bihari Vajpayee, had introduced many schemes to ease the hardships of families who had lost sons or husbands in the Kargil War. Yes, the loss of their brave loved ones couldn't be compensated by any kind of remuneration, but acknowledging their sacrifices and offering support was necessary. The prime minister carried out this welfare with devotion and empathy. Families of martyrs received petrol pumps, cash and houses. But the number of impacted families was much higher than the scope of these schemes. So, one of the most feasible schemes was to provide housing to the families of martyrs and disabled soldiers. The houses were constructed in the sub-city of Dwarka in the heart of Delhi. The prime minister himself came to inaugurate the society, and we received the keys to our house from his noble hands. His presence and speech touched our hearts. Not only the government, but many corporate companies and people of the nation too came forward with welfare schemes, extending their support. We could feel our countrymen with us at every step of the way during our struggles. Akhilesh and I moved to our Dwarka house with our two-and-a-half-year-old daughter and 10-day-old son in our arms.

RE-ATTIRED

Dreams are renewable. No matter our age or condition, there are still untapped possibilities within us and there is new beauty waiting to be born.

Dedication and sincerity towards work are required in every profession, and who carries these qualities better than an army man. Once a soldier, always a soldier. The training he underwent at the NDA, the values instilled in him by the Indian Army, and the experience of the Kargil war provided Akhilesh with a firm base in his leadership journey. The first project he managed at Wipro was an eye-opener for him into the corporate world. It was a huge cultural shock; going from a world where your colleagues would sacrifice their lives for you to a competitive and cut-throat arena of self-promotion. The people were ambitious, skilful and sophisticated, but they did not hesitate to make false commitments, highlight their minor contributions, and take undue credit for work done by their juniors. Everyone was your colleague, but there was no one you could trust. The air-conditioned environment was luxurious but missing brotherhood. Initially, it was challenging for Akhilesh to adjust to that atmosphere. Once, I found him sitting wide awake in the drawing room at midnight. He shared many puzzling incidents from his workplace that were making him uncomfortable. We discussed them until dawn, and decided we would never compromise on our values and instead, endeavour to transform others.

A project was handed over to Akhilesh when its project manager resigned due to many misalignments. The dissatisfied customers were writing complaints to the senior management. Missing milestones and revenue were the main concerns for the company. Sales executives were struggling to get new orders. Overall, the customer experience score was one of the lowest. Akhilesh had a meeting with all the team members and customers to analyse the root cause. After a deep study of the project and conducting detailed meetings, he realized there was a difference of opinion within the team. Everyone was working but not in sync with each other. He applied the lessons he learned in the Indian Army that had proven successful during the Kargil War: team members need to have faith in each other and be completely dedicated for the success of the project. Akhilesh defined new rules where the team goal was ranked above individual goals. He established honesty and transparency within the system, and the customers as pillars of strength for the team. Slowly, he was able to build a team with an aligned focus that worked together to resolve customer complaints and meet the management's revenue expectations.

Soon, Akhilesh's leadership skills, hard work, honesty and sincerity were well recognized. He bagged the Most Promising Manager Award and got promoted to Project Head within a few months. Now, working with a team of the most skilled IT executives, he wished to extend his newly acquired knowledge for the betterment of entire team. Within a year of joining Wipro, he was promoted to National Program Manager. Managing a diversified task force of over 145 technical resources, he was responsible for account management, growth in existing projects and maintaining profitability. In three months, he achieved the lowest attrition, highest customer satisfaction and highest enhanced gross margin. He also achieved zero attrition in all his assigned projects. His supportive attitude provided an unmatched experience to his subordinates and juniors. They couldn't believe their boss was empathetic and yet firm with making decisions and finding solutions to every problem. Akhilesh received the prestigious award for Super Boss of the year, but never adopted the behaviour of a boss. He was always a leader who guided his team in the most crucial circumstances and emerged victorious.

The corporate world is a small one, and excellent resources come into focus quickly. Akhilesh received an offer from Airtel to join them as Deputy General Manager (DGM), Business Excellence. His responsibilities included business processes for projects, service delivery, order fulfilment, customer satisfaction, billing and collections at the national level. There, too, he witnessed a lack of coordination between team executives. People were not willing to understand the other person's point of view. Once again, he applied an important learning from his army days to solve this problem: 'Know your man'. He established a personal rapport with each team member. As a leader, he took responsibility for failures to save his team in front of the management; a gesture that was appreciated by everyone. In the meetings, he highlighted many gaps between the management, customers and the team, and proposed strategies to fill those gaps. Initially, the management and customers were irritated and dissatisfied, but later agreed to work in synchronisation for the betterment of the company. He created transparent project timelines with ownership assigned to each team member. Within six months, his team delivered the most successful projects and was awarded the best project team. His style of working was appreciated at Airtel as well. He became popularly known as the best manager. Soon, he was a source of inspiration to the people around him. Juniors and seniors tried to adopt his working style, and there was a change in the thought process of his co-workers.

Akhilesh never thought of his physical disability as a barrier to success. Rather, he carried his wounds with pride. He realized his most valuable and sharp weapon was now his mind. He kept updating his skills by completing certifications such as Project Management Professional (PMP) and Six Sigma Black Belt, with excellent grades.

Meanwhile, my days and nights just slipped away in the handling of two babies and household chores. I couldn't join a corporate company, as it would keep me away from my kids all day and I had no support at home. I worked on my skills and learned Java, HTML and animation. I even completed my Bachelor of Education (B. Ed) during my struggle with motherhood. I looked for a profession where I could balance my career ambitions as well as take care of my responsibilities at home. So, I devoted myself to learning and sharing knowledge as an educator. Teaching and guiding the younger generation can be a fulfilling use of one's time and resources.

In a couple of years, Akhilesh once again received an offer from his dream company, the Tata Group. I still remember the day he came home and kissed my forehead tenderly. 'Today, I got an offer from Tata Group. Remember when I had met their HR head, Mr Pradhan, and he offered me a job because of my disabilities? I refused the offer back then and told him, "One day you will offer me a job because of my abilities". Today is that day!'

'Wow! Congratulations. Everything is possible if you don't lose hope and keep working towards your goals. And who knows this better than us?' I said as I hugged him.

Akhilesh joined Tata Group as GM and Head, Sales Operations & Business Excellence, within the country. He successfully used the lessons learned from the Kargil War in corporate management. He found similarities between military operations and corporate working; there were obstacles, opportunities and planning for eventualities and contingencies on both fronts. Soon, he was featured in the company's annual magazine. He continued working hard, delivering results and updating his skills. After completing the executive course from Indian Institute of Management (IIM), Ahmedabad, he was made Head of Global Sales Operation and Business Processes for international business. The warrior from the Kargil peaks found this easy in comparison to planning warfare strategies on the battlefield. His leadership skills sent him as Tata Group's top performer to Michigan University, USA, to study management techniques.

The Tata Group acknowledges spouses and families as contributors to the company's growth. As they are the ones who directly support their employees and provide them with the environment to work to their optimum potential. This is similar to the value system of the Indian Army, where wives are an integral part of the organization. In 2009, for the first time, Akhilesh became the recipient of the highest award, Pro-club, which is given to only 1%

of Tata Communications employees across its global workforce. As part of the reward, I joined Akhilesh on an exotic holiday to the beautiful forests of Phinda, South Africa. We were amazed by the beauty of the wildlife: African lions, leopards, elephants and giraffes. With his hard work, intelligence and sincerity, Akhilesh bagged the Pro-club award a few more times. And we experienced the swift winds at the edge of the deep sea fjords of Norway, encompassing the mountains and the gigantic glaciers, and had lunch in the village of the Vikings. We travelled to Switzerland, home to a breathtaking landscape dotted with towering peaks and shimmering lakes; and to Cape Town, South Africa, nestled seductively amidst the sea and the mountains. On our last trip, we went to Livingstone, Zambia, to visit Victoria Falls, one of the seven natural wonders of the world, the most fabulous curtain of falling water in the world. Tata organized our meals, celebrations and award nights in the deep forests, on glaciers and mountain tops and cruise ships. We experienced skydiving, forest safaris, river cruises, river rafting, helicopter rides, the world's highest bungee jump and several more adventures on these holidays. These awards gave us the most exotic vacations and beautiful memories of our life. No monetary compensation could have such a tremendous and motivating impact on the hearts and minds of employees.

We changed the direction of our life, but the passion and core values were still the same. We thanked God for giving us the strength to sail through the rough patches with patience and courage. Capt. Akhilesh is now Vice

President and Head – Global Project Management & Operations in Tata Communications, with 20 years of experience working in multinational companies. I'm a mother of two with 20 years of teaching experience, still working for the integrity and unity of our nation. We have suffered the consequences of the Kargil War and understand the pain that Indian soldiers endure. I established an initiative, Inspiring Mantras, with the objective to bring transformation in the vision, thinking process and actions of our countrymen. This initiative is a tribute to our soldiers, who are role models for the people of India. Because the brave heroes of our defence forces selflessly face enemy bullets, citizens are able to lead peaceful lives. Soldiers come from the same society we live in, but their devotion and sincerity towards their country is much higher. No weather conditions, conflict or confusion can distract them from their goal to protect their motherland. What makes them so strong, so different from others? The discipline, training and environment created by the Indian Army make all the difference. The best warriors of India are not tough bodybuilders, smart managers, fast learners or sharp leaders of the country, but regular, hardworking humans. During the war, they often found themselves physically and emotionally spent. Even when they had nothing left to give, they somehow dug deep into themselves to find the energy to help the soldier next to them. They helped their buddies when they were all surrounded by firing and shelling. They saved their brothers in arms when the sky was full of bullets and the ground littered with mines. When there was no hope of survival, when they were approaching death, when conditions were dragging them away from their loved ones – through it all they found the courage to extend a helping hand to their team members. It was team spirit that won the Kargil War. It was India's true 'United we stand and divided we fall' moment.

Guarding the borders is not the only responsibility that the Indian Army carries out. Time and again, they have come forward to provide respite from insurgencies, terrorism, floods, drought and civil war. Their problem-solving skills and attitude are something each one of us should imbibe. We need to take lessons from soldiers who display the qualities of discipline, earnestness, commitment, unity and loyalty. They ooze with an undying team spirit that is willing to find solutions to any problem. To empower any nation, it is not just a dedicated army that is required to guard the borders but a dedicated workforce to develop the economy, infrastructure, and civil behaviour inside the country. We need to create a dedicated and passionate workforce in civilian societies to steer the country towards peace and prosperity. We need to think and work like our soldiers, and become citizens worth fighting for. Let us live up to the saying: 'Every citizen of the country is a soldier if he intends to be'.

The motivating talks, through Inspiring Mantras, and Capt. Akhilesh's leadership methods gradually began leaving imprints in society. Soon, various companies and universities began inviting him for motivational lectures. He successfully used his experiences from the Kargil War and corporate life to lead many teams of executives on the path of success. He started receiving invitations from national news channels as a regular guest speaker. DD National even created an episode on our life. He became like a torch, spreading light wherever he went. And finally, the moment arrived when he had the honour of being featured in the veterans' tableau during our 70th Republic Day Parade at Rajpath in Delhi for his contribution to the country.

Women are the foundation stones of society. They may not always be visible, but they create the base of any institution, be it family or culture. The strongest defence forts require even stronger foundations. And the same is applied to defence forces. It is not only men who have made this organization so dependable, but even the women who march along with their husbands to fulfil the expectations of our countrymen. We do not receive any training to handle these inconveniences of life. Our nervous systems are sympathetically wired. We access emotions and empathy most effortlessly. It is a mysterious and valuable resource for men, especially with weapons. At the time, it was impossible for me to connect the dots. I would secretly cry in the middle of the night thinking, *Why me*? Life had hit me hard with a ton of bricks. But now, 23 years later, when I look back, I realize that I was a part of a powerful community that made a gentle girl strong enough to support her love in every trial of life. I feel privileged to have served my country as the spouse of an officer who was willing to sacrifice his life for his duty, and I was ready to face life without him so he could fulfil his commitment to the nation. My response to troublesome times has changed. Now I say 'Try me' instead of 'Why me'. In any struggle of life, hold on to your faith. Faith that you will overcome, that God is by your side and that you will be proud of yourself someday. Whatever damage happens, nothing in the universe can stop you from letting go and starting over again. No matter how much it hurts now, someday, you will look back and realize that your struggles changed your life for the better. One day, you will tell the story of how you overcame what you went through. And it will become someone else's survival guide.

Life may throw any adverse situation at you,
It's your choice to face it with a victim's mindset
or a winner's attitude.
That will make all the difference.

LETTERS

22 May 1999

My better half hubby,

This is the third month of our marriage... when I found my world. Miss you.

It's really hard to have you so far away, yet we are a part of each other because of the things we've experienced and the talks we've shared. During a hectic day, when I sit back to relax, thoughts of you come drifting into my mind and fill my world with the warmth of your presence. It is almost as if you are right beside me, but when I turn around, I find myself all alone. I wish you knew how much I want to be with you...

Knowing that we see the same sun in the morning and the same moon at night makes me feel a little closer to you.

Tu jahaan jahaan chalega, Mera saaya saath hoga, *because I am inside you.*

I love you, I miss you, I am with you and you are with me. Love you. Take care.

Hoping that we will be together again very soon.

From yours

Honey

21 June 1999

My dear, dearer, dearest Hubby,

Today is a very nice day. I got your letter. In the morning I woke up and prayed "God, please, today I should receive a letter from Akhilesh" and I got it. I am so happy. Today I have not cried while reading your letter. You must be cheerful while writing it. Hubby, be happy always. Yes, nothing can happen to you. God is with you and my wishes, my prayers and my love are with you and will always be with you.

Hubby, I know you are sincerely performing your duties. But you have to do one thing for me. Just take care of my loving husband. Today, I wanted to ask you, when are you coming home? Without you, this house looks deserted. I feel like I am also on a battlefield where I get messages only a few times. Message from my dear hubby. I know you are working very hard. When you come back, I will take good care of you. I will pamper you. I don't know how is the food there, what do you get to eat? When you come back I will cook food for you and feed you with love. Right now, I can only pray for you. I wish I could have joined the Army as your helper so that I could live by your side always. Leave it, let's talk about togetherness, the season of love and romance.

Your photograph is in front of me, while I am writing you this letter. Seems like you are looking at me. I have kept it on my dressing table near the temple. Whenever I look at you, I feel I have known you for ages. God has created me for you and delivered me to you. Here I want to say please always keep me close to your heart. I love you from the depth of my heart and this is the only job I want to do.

I love you, love you and love you.

Yours always

Shikha

Last letter written by Captain Akhilesh before the suicidal attack of Three Pimples Area.

28 June 1999

Dear Honey

By the time you will get this letter, I will be gone... forever, but my love will stay with you, even if I am not there.

Hope you, mummy, papa, Neeraj and everyone is fine at home.

We are fighting a very difficult war, and everything is in favour of the enemy. They are sitting on the top and firing. The weather is chilly and in minus centigrades on the peaks. We do not carry any food when we go for an attack. We achieved an impossible victory on Tololing but lost some of my friends, officers and Jawans.

Now, we are going for a very critical and challenging attack. I don't know if I will come back alive as we have decided to win, even at the cost of our lives.

This may be my last letter to you, and I am full of emotions and sweet memories. I may not be there, but I always love you. We may not have enough time for each other in this life, but we will meet in the next life. Do not be sad about my death as I have done my duty for my country, army and uniform. Go on with life... Keep smiling. Be proud of what your husband has done for the country. Death may come any time, but we will fight till the end and go down in glory. A chosen few have to make sacrifices so that every Indian can enjoy his freedom and sleep peacefully.

I may not be there to take care of my parents when they grow old, take care of them.

I am keeping your photo in my pocket (blue dress wali) as we prepare for the next attack. We will fight and win for India.

Will always love you in this life and forever.

Always yours.

Hubby

ACKNOWLEDGEMENTS

I started writing this book during the lonely lockdowns caused by the pandemic. The environment of depression and dismay had overwhelmed people across the globe, including me. The sounds of laughter and celebration had converted into silent distances. We were all fighting a war against an invisible enemy, which reminded me of the Kargil war, where the terrain and the enemy were unknown to the Indian soldiers. This motivated me to write about those times to inspire society to develop a never-give-up attitude.

During this journey, I met the most reliable, wonderful and positive people, many of whom I am still in touch with and who will remain a part of my life forever. The first two people who read this story were Mrs Kanupriya Rathor and Mrs Neili Randhawa, who laid the foundation for this book. Ms Varsha Naik did the initial editing with dedication. My daughter, Hirushi Saxena, an excellent creative writer, helped me with the flow of the story. Mrs Tripti Pandey helped me sift through my memories. Dipti Patel came as an angel and took my story to the publisher. Swarnima Narayan, commissioning editor at Hachette India, liked my writing and story and gave me the opportunity to create my identity in the world of words. Sonali Jindal patiently worked on my manuscript to polish and present it to the readers. Parul Sharma, Gia Claudette Fernandes and Pritsikha Anil scanned the manuscript thoroughly. Anubha Jain creatively designed the cover page and gave a face to this book.

My sincere thanks to our source of inspiration General Ved Prakash Malik, Ex–Army Chief, under whose leadership the Indian army could achieve success in the ruthless Kargil war. My heart-filled gratitude to Mrs Ranjana Malik, Ex-President AWWA, who has gone through those difficult times, shared pain and pride, and been a strong motherly support. I am grateful to Ex–Air Chief Marsal B.S. Dhanoa, who stood beside his war buddy, Capt. Akhilesh during the war and continues to do so till today. There are many more army officers, soldiers and friends who were a part of the attacks; some are still serving, some have left the service, and some have left for the heavenly abode. Their memories and sacrifices for the nation will continue to inspire coming generations.

And finally, the man I respect, adore and love the most, my husband Capt. Akhilesh, an Indian Army officer, a Kargil war veteran and the source of this story. He narrated the minutest of details, extending his first-hand experience to me. I am proud and grateful that God has chosen me to be his life partner.

No success is without a team. The book you are holding contains the hard work, dedication and support of so many. This is not just a book but the experience and lessons of a lifetime with which to defeat any adverse times we face.